# Scientific and Technical
# Text Processing
# Using WordStar

# Scientific and Technical Text Processing Using WordStar

## A Guide for Beginning and Advanced Users

### Charles P. McKeague

**McGraw-Hill Book Company**

New York   St. Louis   San Francisco   Auckland   Bogotá
Hamburg   Johannesburg   London   Madrid
Mexico   Montreal   New Delhi   Panama
Paris   São Paulo   Singapore
Sydney   Tokyo   Toronto

Library of Congress Cataloging in Publication Data

McKeague, Charles P.
  Scientific and technical text processing using
WordStar.

  Includes index.
  1. Technical writing—Data processing.   2. WordStar
(Computer program)   3. Word processing.   I. Title.
T11.M368   1985        808′.0666021        84-20193
ISBN 0-07-044391-2

1234567890   DOC/DOC   898765

*The editors for this book were Stephen Guty and Chet Gottfried,
the designer was Naomi Auerbach, and the production
supervisor was Sally Fliess. It was set in Century Schoolbook
by University Graphics, Inc.*
*Printed and bound by R. R. Donnelley & Sons Company.*

# Contents

# Preface

I began shopping for a word processing system after signing a contract to write a trigonometry book. I spent more than 6 months looking at computers and talking with people about word processing programs. Although none of the people I talked with had any experience with the kind of word processing I had to do, the people who knew about word processors thought that WordStar would be the program to buy. They didn't know whether WordStar could do what I wanted it to do, but if WordStar couldn't do it, then none of the other programs could either.

As it turned out, WordStar is exactly the program I needed. I am still surprised by some of the things it can do. And contrary to what I had read about it, WordStar is very easy to use, once you become familiar with it.

I learned to use WordStar by reading the manual. Since I didn't have any prior experience with word processing, it took me a few months to learn it well. I realize now that I could have shortened that learning process.

The first thing that could have saved me some time was a simple, step-by-step guide to take me through the basic editing commands.

Once I had learned the basics of text entering and editing, I could have used some examples and hints on how to do technical word processing efficiently. WordStar is capable of doing some very complicated text formatting. Some of this kind of formatting can be accomplished in more than one way, and many times there are shortcuts that will save time when doing so. In my case, it took me a while to discover these shortcuts. For example, in my trigonometry book, there are hundreds of places in which a degree symbol, as in 45°, occurs. There are a couple of ways to obtain a degree symbol with WordStar, depending on the printer in use. No matter which method is used, at least four control characters appear on the screen for every degree symbol to be printed. Entering and proofreading a screen full of control characters can be a problem. It took me two chapters of trigonometry before I realized I could simply type an asterisk in place of a degree symbol and then use the find and replace command to replace each asterisk with the sequence of control characters necessary to print a degree symbol. Not only does this save time in typing, but I never have to worry about whether or not I have typed the correct codes for the degree symbol.

The first chapter of this book contains the kind of material I would have liked to have when I was just beginning to use WordStar. It has the information a first-time WordStar user needs to get WordStar up and running, plus it takes the user through the basic WordStar editing commands in a step-by-step manner.

The rest of the book contains information on the more advanced WordStar commands. In addition, it covers in some detail the combination of commands you need to use to format text of a scientific or mathematical nature. There are separate chapters on equations and fractions, as well as examples of how to format some of the formulas you find in chemistry and physics. Essentially, this part of the book is what I needed most after I had learned to use the basic editing commands and was ready to try the more complicated formatting procedures.

Although this book contains all the information you need to become an expert at using WordStar for normal word processing and technical word processing, it does not contain each and every detail associated with the WordStar commands. There are some things covered in the WordStar manual that are not covered here.

## How to Use This Book

If you have a version of WordStar that has been installed for your computer system (your terminal and your printer), and you know how to get WordStar on the screen but are inexperienced with WordStar, then you should begin by reading Chapter 1.

If you do not know what an installed version of WordStar is, you need to read through the installation manual that accompanies WordStar or talk to the dealer who sold you WordStar.

If you have had some experience with WordStar and are familiar with the WordStar commands for moving the cursor and inserting and deleting text, you will probably want to start with Chapter 2 or Chapter 4, depending on how well you know WordStar.

If you are an experienced WordStar user who just needs some help with formatting complicated text, you may want to look through the later chapters in the book or go to the index to look up the topic with which you need help.

## A Note on Terminology

If you are just getting started using a computer and word processor, there will be some terms and vocabulary that you will not understand. The glossary at the back of the book lists some of the most common words and phrases found in word processing. When you run across a word you do not recognize, take the time to turn to the glossary and see what it means.

## Printers

There are some important functions that your printer should be able to perform if it is going to print text that contains scientific and mathematical symbols. Most important is that your printer be able to do exponents (superscripts) and subscripts. If your printer is capable of producing exponents and subscripts, it will do so either by rolling the carriage up or down a half line or by using special characters already programmed into it. For some notes on how to install your printer so that you can take advantage of these, and other, features, turn to Appendixes B and C.

## A Note on My Computers

The main system I use has three components. The computer itself is an SB-80 computer manufactured by Colonial Data in Hamden, Connecticut. It is a single-board computer that contains a Z80A microprocessor and 64K of memory and holds a total of 1.2 megabytes of storage on two 8-inch disk drives. My terminal is a TeleVideo 950. I have two printers: a letter-quality NEC 5530 and a dot-matrix Epson FX-80. My system works very well. I have never had problems with any part of it.

## Acknowledgments

There are several people who deserve a sincere thank-you for their help with the production of this book. My editor at McGraw-Hill, Stephen Guty, and I have worked on a number of projects over the past 7 years. As always, it has been a pleasure to work with him. Lori Lawson helped enter the manuscript in my computer. She is an expert at using WordStar and always does a fine job. Lee Welch reviewed the final draft of the manuscript and used it to learn WordStar for himself. His comments and suggestions were very helpful. The people at Peripheral Vision Company reviewed an earlier version of the manuscript and made a number of useful suggestions also. Finally, my wife, Diane, and my children, Patrick and Amy, have once again been a source of encouragement in getting me to finish the manuscript for this book.

# Scientific and Technical
# Text Processing
# Using WordStar

# 1

# Getting Started

In this first chapter we introduce you to some of the most often used WordStar editing commands. If you are already familiar with WordStar, you may want to move on to Chapter 2, or even Chapter 4. On the other hand, if you are a first-time user of WordStar, or have used WordStar only occasionally, this chapter, and the two chapters that follow, should be of particular value to you.

We begin this chapter by explaining some of the things you will see when you first look at WordStar on the screen of your computer. Then we show you how to open a file and have you type in a short paragraph. From there we cover most of the commands used for editing and show you how to save a file. The chapter ends with a look at the WordStar menus. As you will see as you progress through the book, many of the commands covered in this chapter are covered in more detail later on in the book. For the moment, we are just trying to become familiar with WordStar and are not particularly concerned with all the details contained in the specific commands. Also, if you find some terms or phrases in this chapter that are unfamiliar to you, take the time to look them up in the glossary at the back of the book.

## 1.1 Opening a File, Entering Text, and Saving a File

We will assume that you have made one or more backup copies of the version of WordStar that you purchased and that you are not working with the original. (You should always work with copies of your original programs, never with the originals themselves. It is also a good idea to store your original programs in a different place from where you store your copies.) Further, we are assuming that you are using an installed version

1

of WordStar. That is, you have run the installation program that came with WordStar to customize WordStar to your terminal and printer.

Insert your diskette containing WordStar into drive A and press the RESET button, or whatever you need to do on your computer to get the familar A> prompt on your screen. Then type DIR and press the RETURN key to obtain a directory of all the files on your diskette. On some computers the RETURN key is labeled CR, ENTER, RET, or ↵, as on the IBM Personal Computer. In order to run WordStar, you must have these three files on the diskette in drive A: WS.COM, WSOVLY1.OVR, WSMSGS.OVR. If one or more of these files are not on the diskette in drive A, then WordStar will not run. If you are running WordStar under CP/M-86 or MS-DOS, these files may have slightly different names.

To call up WordStar—that is, to run the WordStar word processing program—type WS and then press the RETURN key. The CP/M prompt will roll off the screen, and you will see a message similar to this and, possibly, a copyright message as well.

```
WordStar installed for
            TeleVideo 950 Terminal
            NEC 5510/5520 printer
            No communications protocol
            CP/M list device (LST:)
```

After a few seconds these messages will be replaced by what is called the *opening menu,* or *no-file menu,* depending on which version of WordStar you have. (Earlier versions up to 3.0 call it the no-file menu, while versions higher that 3.0 call it the opening menu.) The opening, or no-file, menu is shown in Figure 1.

```
              < < < O P E N I N G  M E N U  > > >
     --- Preliminary  Commands ---   --File Commands--    -System Commands-
   L  Change logged disk drive   |                    |  R  Run a program
   F  File directory   now ON    |  P  Print a file   |  X  EXIT to system
   H  Set Help level             |                    |
     ---Commands to open a file--- |  E  RENAME a file | -WordStar Options-
      D  Open a document file     |  O  COPY a file    |  M  Run MailMerge
      N  Open a non-document file |  Y  DELETE a file  |  S  Run SpellStar

   DIRECTORY of disk A:
   EXAMPLE1.TXT   EXAMPLE1.BAK
```

**Figure 1**   Opening, or no-file, menu.

The commands available under the opening menu are grouped together in categories. (The first of these categories is titled *Preliminary Commands.*) We will explain all the commands on the opening menu at the end of this chapter. For now, we want to get started word processing, so we will go directly to the command to open a file.

Look at the commands available under the *Commands to open a file* category; they are D and N. The phrase to the right of each letter explains what pressing that letter will do. Before we go any further, let's take a moment to explain the format we use to introduce new commands.

In this book, we introduce and explain each WordStar command by first listing the command and its function and then explaining the command in more detail with a paragraph or two under the heading *Comments.* Many times we will follow the Comments section with a section entitled *Example,* which will further illustrate the command in question by showing an example of how that command is used. Here is our first WordStar command explained with this format.

| Command from opening menu | Function |
|:---:|:---:|
| D | Open a document file |
| N | Open a nondocument file |

**Comments.**    Basically, the D command is used for word processing and the N command is used for writing programs. If you are reading this book, you are probably interested in word processing, so we will cover the D command only. When you press the D from the no-file menu, WordStar will prompt (ask) you for the name of the file you want to open. At the same time, it will tell you what kind of file names you can use.

**Example.**    With the opening (or no-file) menu showing on your screen, press D (it doesn't have to be a capital D) to open a document file, and watch how WordStar fills your screen with information on how to name the file you want to open, and then prompts you for that name. Next, type EXAMPLE1.TXT and press the RETURN key on your keyboard. After doing so, you should see Figure 2 (on the next page) on your screen.

Your screen is now composed of four parts: the *status line,* the *main menu,* the *ruler line,* and the *text area.*

**Status line.**    The top line on your screen is called the *status line.* It begins with the name of the file you are working on. The file name is preceded by the letter of the disk drive on which the file is located. If you have followed the instructions so far, this should be drive A. After the file name is the page number of the file, and after that is the line number and column number of the present cursor position. Finally, the status line tells you when you are in the INSERT ON mode (explained in Section 1.3). As you type text onto the screen, the status line will be continually updated to reflect the current position of the cursor (line and column number).

*The main menu.* The main menu gives you a summary of the commands used most often. They include commands for moving the cursor, deleting text, and turning the INSERT on or off. It also shows you how to access the other menus available under WordStar. In a moment, we explain these commands in more detail.

*The ruler line.* The *ruler line* shows you the current settings for the left and right margins, as well as the tab stops. WordStar usually comes with the left margin set at column 1 and the right margin set at column 65. The first tab stop is at column 6, and the others are every five spaces after that.

*The text area.* The blank area following the ruler line is called the *text area*. It is the part of the screen on which the characters you type on the keyboard appear.

```
    B:LETTER.TXT    PAGE 1 LINE 1  COL 01            INSERT ON
                  < < <    M A I N    M E N U    > > >
    --Cursor Movement--  | -Delete- |  -Miscellaneous-  | -Other Menus-
^S char left ^D char right |^G  Char  | ^I Tab    ^B Reform| (from Main only)
^A word left ^F word right |DEL chr lf| ^V INSERT ON/OFF   |^J Help  ^K Block
^E line  up  ^X line down  |^T word rt|^L Find/Replce again|^Q Quick ^P Print
    --Scrolling--          |^Y line   |RETURN End paragraph|^O Onscreen
^W up line    ^Z down line |          | ^N Insert a RETURN |
^R up screen ^C down screen|          | ^U Stop a command  |
L----!----!----!----!----!----!----!----!----!----!----!--------R
```

**Figure 2**   Main menu.

Now type in the following paragraph. Don't worry about making mistakes while you type. That is, don't try to go back and fix them just yet. Also, do not touch the RETURN key until you have typed in the complete paragraph. As you type, notice how the column number on the status line changes each time you type a new character. Notice also what happens as you type past the right margin (column 65): WordStar automatically aligns your text at column 65 (which is called right justification) and takes words that will not fit on the current line and places them at the beginning of the next line (which is called word wrapping).

This is a sample paragraph I am typing so that I can get used to
some of the WordStar editing commands.  When I have typed the
whole paragraph, I will save it.  Then I will try some of the
WordStar editing commands that let me insert and delete text.  I
am not too concerned with whether or not I make some mistakes.
In fact, if I do make a mistake or two, I will fix them when I
edit the paragraph.  After all, that is one of the advantages of
using a word processor rather than a typewriter.  After I have
done some editing and reformatting of this paragraph, I will move
parts of it from one place to another.

The next thing to do is to save the file you have just typed. You can use one of three commands to do so. These commands are the first commands that require use of the CONTROL key on your keyboard. Note that this key may be labeled CTRL, CNTL, ALT, or ↑ (an up arrow), depending on the kind of keyboard you have. The symbol we use for it is ^, and we refer to it as the CONTROL key. The CONTROL key works in the same manner as the SHIFT key; it gives an alternate meaning to the key you press while it is held down.

| Command | Function |
|---------|----------|
| ^KS | Save and continue editing |
| ^KD | Save and return to opening menu |
| ^KX | Save and return to operating system |

**Comments.**  To give any of these commands, you must hold down the CONTROL key, and while doing so type K (it doesn't have to be a capital K), followed by S, D, or X. (Don't do it yet.) It is not necessary to hold down the CONTROL key while you type the second letter of each command. If more that 1 second goes by between the time you type ^K and the next letter, WordStar will put the K menu on the screen over the main menu. Notice that the command you choose to save your file depends on what you want to do after you have saved it. The first command, ^KS, is the command to do what is known as a *temporary save* of the file you are working on. With this command, WordStar will save the file and then let you continue editing it. The second save command, ^KD, saves the file you are working on and then returns you to the opening (or no-file) menu. From there you can open another file, print a file, or do any of the things available under the opening menu. The third save command, ^KX, saves your file and then exits WordStar and takes you back to your operating system.

**Example.**   Let's do a temporary save of the text you just typed. With the text from EXAMPLE1.TXT showing on your screen, give the first of the save commands, ^KS. (Remember, hold down the CONTROL key while you type K.) Now wait while WordStar saves your file to the diskette in drive A. When WordStar has finished, you will see your file come back on the screen along with this message:

```
TO RETURN CURSOR TO POSITION BEFORE SAVE,
TYPE ^QP BEFORE TYPING ANYTHING ELSE.
```

As this message indicates, typing ^QP before you type anything else will return the cursor to where it was before you gave the save command.

**Important Note.**   Nothing you type on your screen is saved to your diskette until you tell WordStar to save it. If you have been typing away for 15 minutes or so and the power to your computer goes out, you will lose everything you have typed, unless you have saved it. For this reason, I do a temporary save, ^KS, of the file I am working on every 5 or 10 minutes.

Before we move on to the next section, give the command to save and return to the opening menu, ^KD. When the opening menu comes back on your screen, notice that, in addition to the file EXAMPLE1.TXT, there is a new file, EXAMPLE1.BAK, listed on the directory. Every time you give one of the commands to save a file, WordStar will take the previous copy of that file and rename it with the file extension .BAK, before it saves the file you are working on under the original name you gave it. This way you always have a backup copy of the file you are saving.

## 1.2  Moving the Cursor and Scrolling

In this section we cover the commands that move the cursor around the screen. As we cover the different commands that control the movement of the cursor, you should try each of them yourself. You want these commands to become second nature to you. That is, you want to know them so well that you don't have to look them up to use them.

To begin this section, open the file EXAMPLE1.TXT that you typed in and saved in Section 1.1, if it is not already on your screen. (From the opening, or no-file, menu type D to open a file. When WordStar asks for the name of the file to edit, type EXAMPLE1.TXT, followed by RETURN.)

Notice on your main menu that the first category of commands is *cursor movement*. To move the cursor around the screen you use these commands. For example, to move the cursor up one character, you press ^E, which means you depress the CONTROL key on your keyboard (remember that it may be labeled CTRL, CNTL, ALT, or ↑), and while holding down the CONTROL key, you also press the E key (it doesn't have to be a capital E).

| Command | Function |
|---------|----------|
| ^S | Cursor left one character |
| ^D | Cursor right one character |
| ^E | Cursor up one character |
| ^X | Cursor down one character |

**Comments.** The keys S, D, E, and X when used in conjunction with the CONTROL key are called the *cursor control keys*. Notice that they form a diamond on your keyboard. The position of each key in the diamond indicates the direction in which the cursor will move if that key is used in conjunction with the CONTROL key.

To Move the Cursor One Character

up

**E**

left    **S D**    right

**X**

down

**Important Note.** You can only use the cursor control keys to move the cursor over lines and spaces on which you have already typed. If you try to use the cursor control keys to advance the cursor past the last character you typed, it will not move. Also, the arrow keys on your keyboard may not work while using WordStar. On some computers, like the IBM Personal Computer, WordStar is installed so that the arrow keys on the keyboard have the same function as the cursor control keys explained above. But on many other computers and terminals that is not the case.

You can move the cursor left and right along a line faster with the following two commands:

| Command | Function |
|---------|----------|
| ^F | Cursor right one word |
| ^A | Cursor left one word |

**Comments.**  I use these commands quite often. Each command moves the cursor from its present position to the beginning of the word to its right or left.

The previous six commands show you how to move the cursor around the screen. The next four commands show how to move the screen instead of the cursor. They are the commands for scrolling.

## Scrolling

The WordStar commands that move the screen up or down one line (or more) at a time are as follows:

| Command | Function |
|---------|----------|
| ^W | Scroll screen up one line |
|    | (Moves text down one line) |
| ^Z | Scroll screen down one line |
|    | (Moves text up one line) |
| ^R | Scroll screen up one screen |
|    | (Moves text down one screen) |
| ^C | Scroll screen down one screen |
|    | (Moves text up one screen) |

**Comments.**  On the IBM Personal Computer, the ^R command can also be accessed by pressing the key labeled Pg up on the numeric key pad, when the number lock is on. Likewise, pressing Pg down is equivalent to the ^C command. Note that this is only true if your WordStar has been installed to run on the IBM Personal Computer. For the last two commands above, one screen is about eighteen lines. Try these commands, and don't worry if you scroll the text you have typed completely off the screen. You haven't lost it; it's just not in view.

## Further Cursor Movement

The cursor can be moved to the beginning of your file, end of your file, or to the beginning or end of a line with the commands that follow.

| Command | Function |
|---------|----------|
| ^QS | Cursor to beginning of line |
| ^QD | Cursor to end of line |
| ^QR | Cursor to top of file |
| ^QC | Cursor to end of file |

**Comments.**  On the IBM Personal Computer, function key F9 performs the same task as the command ^QR, and function key F10 is equivalent to the ^QC command. Also, remember that when you type these two-letter commands, you need to hold down the CONTROL key while you type the first letter, but not the second, and the letters you type do not have to be capital letters. I didn't use these commands when I was first learning WordStar; but now that I know about them, I use them all the time.

### Further Scrolling

These commands will instruct WordStar to scroll continuously through the current file one line at a time.

| Command | Function |
|---------|----------|
| ^QZ | Scroll text up continuously |
| ^QW | Scroll text down continuously |

**Comments.** You can vary the speed at which the continuous scrolling takes place by typing any of the numbers 1 through 9. The number 1 will give you the fastest scrolling and 9 will give you the slowest. WordStar starts scrolling at 3.

## 1.3 Editing a File: Inserting Text and Paragraph Re-form

In this section we explain some of the basic editing techniques available with WordStar. To begin, call up the file EXAMPLE1.TXT that you were working with in the previous section (from the opening menu, press D and then type EXAMPLE1.TXT and press the RETURN key). As we proceed through the commands that follow, be sure to try them yourself. The more times you use a command, the easier it will be to remember it and the more comfortable you will be with it.

### INSERT ON and INSERT OFF

The first command we cover in this section is very useful for editing. It is the command that puts WordStar into one of two modes or states: INSERT ON or INSERT OFF.

| Command | Function |
|---------|----------|
| ^V | INSERT on/off |

**Comments.** With the INSERT on, you can insert text (including blank spaces) in a file you have already typed. When WordStar is in this state, any character you type will be inserted in your text at the cursor position, moving the characters to the right of the cursor position one more space to the right. When the INSERT is off, you will type over the text at the current cursor position. When the INSERT is on, you will see the words *INSERT ON* at the top of your screen on the right side of the status line. Further, when the INSERT is off, the right of this part of the status line will be blank. Also, on the IBM PC, the key labeled *Ins on* has the same function as ^V.

**Example.**  Assuming you have EXAMPLE1.TXT from the previous section on your screen, press ^V two or three times and watch the right side of the status line to see how the words INSERT ON are alternately showing and not showing as you change back and forth between the two editing states. With WordStar in the INSERT ON mode, move the cursor to the beginning of your file, if it is not already there, and type the word *Example*. Notice how WordStar moves the rest of the characters on the line to the right as you type. Next, press the TAB key (labeled ⇆ on the IBM Personal Computer), and notice what happens. (If you do not have a TAB key on your keyboard, give the command ^I.) Now move the cursor to the beginning of the second sentence. With the cursor on the letter W of the word *When,* press ^V to turn the INSERT off. Now type the word *After.* If you need to insert a space following the word *After,* turn the INSERT back on and press the space bar. Finally, with the INSERT on, move the cursor to the beginning of the third sentence, and press RETURN, and then press the TAB key. You should now have two paragraphs, where you had just one previously.

### Re-forming Paragraphs

After completing the example above, you will notice that your right margin is no longer aligned. WordStar will fix this for you with the next command. It is the command to re-form a paragraph.

| Command | Function |
|---------|----------|
| ^B | Re-form paragraph |

**Comments.**  When this command is given, WordStar will realign the right side of the paragraph containing the cursor, from the line containing the cursor to the end of the paragraph. The alignment will be according to the current setting of the right margin.

**Example.**  Move the cursor to the beginning of the file EXAMPLE1.TXT that you edited in the example above, and then give the ^B command. The first paragraph will be realigned on the right, and the cursor will end up at the beginning of the second paragraph. WordStar may stop the realignment process and ask you a question about hyphenation. This is called *hyphenation help,* and we discuss the options available with it when we cover re-forming paragraphs in more detail in Chapter 3. For now, simply give the ^B command again to continue the realignment process.

## 1.4 Further Editing: Deleting Text

WordStar has a number of commands that allow you to delete text. You can delete a single character, a word, a line, or the line to the right (or left) of the cursor. (And there are commands that allow you to delete more than a line at a time. But we will wait to cover them until the next section.) Here are the commands for deleting a line or less of text.

| Command | Function |
| --- | --- |
| DEL | Backspace and delete |
| ^G | Delete a character |
| ^T | Delete a word |
| ^Y | Delete a line |
| ^QY | Delete to end of line |
| ^Q DEL | Delete to beginning of line |

**Comments.** The first command, DEL, stands for the DELETE key which you may or may not have on your keyboard (sometimes it is labeled RUB or RUBOUT). If you have it, pressing it will move the cursor back one space and then delete any character at that position. The next command, ^G, will delete the character at the cursor position and move the rest of the characters on that line one space to the left. The second command, ^T, will delete the word to the right of the cursor position, if the cursor is on a nonblank character (if the word is followed by a punctuation mark, WordStar will delete the punctuation mark also). If the cursor is on a blank space, this command will delete the rest of the spaces from the cursor position to the next nonblank space. The ^Y command will delete all characters on the line containing the cursor and move the remaining lines in the file up one line. The ^QY command deletes all characters on the line from the cursor position to the end of the line. The last command requires use of the DELETE key. When used, it deletes all characters from the cursor position to the beginning of the line, moving the cursor and the characters on the line to its right to the beginning of the line.

**Example.** If not already on the screen, call up the file EXAMPLE1.TXT that you were working with in the previous section. Move the cursor to the beginning of the second sentence. Now give each of the commands listed above, one at a time, and notice what happens on the screen. Next, move the cursor to the bottom of the file with ^QC. Now press the RETURN key a few times. The cursor should move down a few lines and WordStar should place some carriage return symbols on the right of the screen. Move the cursor back up to the line containing the first of these carriage returns, and give the command to delete a character, ^G. Notice how WordStar deletes the carriage return symbol. Delete the rest of them. Now move down a line and type the word *equation*. Move the cursor to the beginning of equation, and with the INSERT on, insert a few spaces in front of it. Now delete these spaces. I find this combination of deleting and inserting text very useful for positioning equations and other dis-played text on a line. When you have finished practicing these commands, give the command ^KQ. This is the command to abandon the file without saving any changes you have made. (I use this command after I have been showing my friends some of the things that I can do with WordStar. With this command, I can call up a file and make all kinds of changes in it and then abandon it without making those those changes permanent.)

## 1.5  Block Operations: Inserting and Deleting Larger Amounts of Text

Although much of the editing you do is centered around changes in single characters, words, or lines, there are times when you will want to edit larger amounts of text. WordStar will let you manipulate larger blocks of text, but you must first mark the block of text you want to work with. You do so with the following commands:

| Command | Function |
|---------|----------|
| ^KB | Mark the beginning of a block |
| ^KK | Mark the end of a block |

**Comments.**  On the IBM Personal Computer, pressing function key F7 is equivalent to the giving the first command, ^KB, while function key F8 is equivalent to the second command, ^KK. When you give the command ^KB, WordStar will insert ⟨B⟩ at the cursor position. What happens when you give the command ^KK depends on the kind of terminal you have. If your terminal is capable of *highlighting* (some text is lighter than other text) or *reverse video* (black characters on a light background), you will see the block you have just marked displayed that way. If your ter-minal is not capable of highlighting or reverse video, then you will see ⟨K⟩ displayed at the end of each line of the block and a ⟨B⟩ displayed at the beginning of each line in your block. (Note that some versions of WordStar will display only the first ⟨B⟩ and the last ⟨K⟩ of the marked block.)

**Example.** Using the file EXAMPLE1.TXT that you have been working with, move the cursor to the beginning of any sentence and give the command to mark the beginning of a block, ^KB. Now move the cursor one space past the end of that sentence, and give the command to mark the end of a block, ^KK. You should now see how your terminal marks a block of text. Leave EXAMPLE1.TXT for a moment and read through the next commands.

### Playing with the Marked Block

After you have marked a block of text, you can do a number of things with it, as the following commands indicate.

| Command | Function |
|---------|----------|
| ^KV | Move marked block to cursor position |
| ^KC | Copy marked block |
| ^KY | Delete marked block |
| ^KH | Hide block markers |

**Comments.** Both of the first two commands will move a marked block of text. The first one deletes the marked block from its original position, while the second one leaves it where it is.

**Example.** Try the first of the above commands on the block of text you just marked by first moving the cursor to the end of the file, ^QC, and then giving command ^KV. Now move to the end of the file, again with ^QC, and give the second command ^KC. Repeat this process until you have tried each of the commands. When you have finished, give the command to abandon the file, ^KQ.

## 1.6  The Opening (or No-File) Menu Revisited

In this section we will simply list the commands that are available under the opening (or no-file) menu. To make the best use of this section, you should have the opening menu showing on your screen. (From A> prompt, simply type WS and then press the RETURN key. After a few moments the opening menu will appear on the screen.)

The commands available on the opening menu are grouped together in categories. The first of these categories is entitled *Preliminary Commands*. Look at the letters in the left-hand column of this category: L, F, and H. The phrase to the right of each of these letters explains what pressing that letter will do. A short explanation of each of these commands follows.

**Preliminary Commands**

| Command from opening menu | Function |
|:---:|:---:|
| L | Change logged disk drive |

**Comments.** In computer language, the logged disk drive is the disk drive the computer is working from. Right now, the logged disk drive is drive A (assuming you have just called up WordStar from the diskette in drive A). If you call up WordStar from a diskette in drive A and then give this command, WordStar will look for the files you want to open, and save the files you want to save, on the diskette in drive B. This is helpful if your system does not have enough space on the drives to hold both WordStar and the files you want to work with.

| Command from opening menu | Function |
|:---:|:---:|
| F | File directory on or off |

**Comments.** Pressing F will turn the file directory off. Pressing it a second time will turn it back on. Press F.(It can be a capital F, a lowercase f, or ^F.)

| Command from opening menu | Function |
|:---:|:---:|
| H | Set help level |

**Comments.** The "help level" you select under this command is the degree to which WordStar gives you explanations for the commands you initiate. The help level is usually in terms of the menus that will be displayed by WordStar on your screen. Pressing H will cause WordStar to display the help level options available to you. Here they are as you would see them displayed on the screen:

```
  H        editing no file

  HELP LEVELS
    3  all menus and explanations displayed
    2  main editing memu (1-control-char commands) suppressed
    1  prefix menus (2-character commands) also suppressed
    0  command explanations (including this) also suppressed

  CURRENT HELP LEVEL IS 3

  ENTER Space OR NEW HELP LEVEL (0, 1, 2, OR 3):

  partial DIRECTORY of disk A:  ^Z=scroll up
```

The default help level is 3. At this help level, WordStar displays the maximum amount of information it is capable of displaying. Most people use help level 3 when they are learning WordStar and help levels 2 or 1 after they have become more familiar with WordStar.

The commands to open a file are in our next category of opening menu commands. Since we covered these commands previously in Section 1.1, we will simply list them here.

### Commands to Open a File

| Command for opening menu | Function |
|---|---|
| D | Open a document file |
| N | Open a nondocument file |

### System Commands

These two commands allow you to do things external to WordStar. The first command takes you out of WordStar and back to your operating system. The second command allows you to run a program external to WordStar, like STAT.COM.

| Command from opening menu | Function |
|---|---|
| R | Run a program |

**Comments.** If you press R from the opening menu, WordStar will ask you for the name of the program you want to run. The program must have the file extension COM. A common program to run from this command is the

CP/M program STAT.COM, which tells you how much space you have left on the diskette.

| Command from opening menu | Function |
|:---:|:---:|
| X | Exit to system |

**Comments.**   Giving this command will take you out of WordStar, back to your operating system.

### WordStar Operations

These two commands allow you to run the two programs that are integrated with WordStar but separate from WordStar. The first is Mail-Merge and the second is SpellStar.

| Command from opening menu | Function |
|:---:|:---:|
| M | Run MailMerge |

**Comments.**   MailMerge is a program that can be purchased to accompany WordStar. It allows you to create and print letters and mailing-label lists, among other things.

| Command from opening menu | Function |
|:---:|:---:|
| S | Run SpellStar |

**Comments.**   SpellStar is also a program written to accompany WordStar. It is used to check the spelling of the words in the files you have created. It is usually purchased separately from WordStar.

### File Commands

These commands allow you to print, rename, copy, or delete a file you have already created and saved. In each case WordStar will prompt you with the name of the file you want to do these things to.

| Command from opening menu | Function |
|:---:|:---:|
| P | Print a file |

**Comments.** This is one of the most widely used commands from the opening menu. It is the command that lets you print a file on your printer. It is explained in more detail in Section 3.1.

| Command from opening menu | Function |
|:---:|:---:|
| E | Rename a file |

**Comments.** There are times when you will want to rename a file you have already created. (For example, if you want to edit one of your backup files that has the extension BAK, you will first have to give it another name, because WordStar will not open files with the extension BAK.)

| Command from opening menu | Function |
|:---:|:---:|
| O | Copy a file |

**Comments.** This command allows you to copy a file on the diskette in drive A to the diskette in drive B (or from drive B to drive A), without having to exit to the system and use the PIP or COPY commands.

| Command from opening menu | Function |
|:---:|:---:|
| Y | Delete a file |

**Comments.** Use this command with caution. It will delete the file under the file name you specify. Once it is gone, it is gone for good.

## 1.7 The Other WordStar Menus

WordStar is sometimes referred to as a *menu-driven word processor*. The reason is that each and every command available from WordStar is listed on one of the WordStar menus. So far, we have covered the commands accessed through the opening menu and the main menu in detail. As we progress through the book, we will cover the remaining commands and the menus on which they are listed. In the meantime, you may want to look over the remaining menus to get some feel for the way in which WordStar is organized. What follows is a list of the menus we will cover in the next few chapters, along with a short explanation of the types of commands that are available under those menus. To begin this section, open the file EXAMPLE1.TXT that we have worked with previously.

## The On-screen Menu

To get WordStar to place the on-screen menu on your screen, give the command ^O from any menu except the opening menu. Pressing the space bar after the on-screen menu appears on the screen will return you to the main menu. From the on-screen menu you can reset the margins, the line spacing, and the tab stops, among other things. Generally, the commands you give from the on-screen menu affect the way in which the text appears on your screen. That is why it is called the *onscreen menu*. Figure 3 shows what it looks like when you see it on your screen.

```
^O      B:LETTER.TXT    PAGE 1 LINE 1    COL 01        INSERT ON
                    < < <  O N S C R E E N   M E N U  > > >
   -Margins & Tabs-  | -Line Functions- |  --More Toggles--  |  -Other Menus-
 L Set left margin  |C Center text      |J Justify    now ON | (from Main only)
 R Set right margin |S Set line spacing |V Vari-tabs  now ON |^J Help  ^K Block
 X Release margins  |                   |H Hyph-help  now ON |^Q Quick ^P Print
 I Set  N Clear tab |    --Toggles--    |E Soft hyph now OFF |^O Onscreen
 G Paragraph tab    |W Wrd wrap  now ON |D Prnt disp  now ON |Space bar returns
 F Ruler from line  |T Rlr line  now ON |P Pge break  now ON |you to Main Menu.
 L----!----!----!----!----!----!----!----!----!----!----!--------R
```

**Figure 3**  The on-screen menu.

## The Print Menu

Giving the command ^P from any menu except the opening menu and the print menu will cause the print menu to appear on your screen. Once it is showing on your screen, pressing the space bar will return you to the main menu. Generally, the print menu contains those commands that will send instructions to your printer when you are printing a file you have created. From the print menu you can instruct your printer to underline text and print text in bold type, among other things. The print menu will look like Figure 4 when you see it on your screen.

```
^P      B:LETTER.TXT    PAGE 1  LINE 1   COL 01       INSERT ON
                    < < <      P R I N T   M E N U    > > >
   ------- Special Effects ------- |  -Printing  Changes- |  -Other Menus-
 (begin and end) |  (one time each) |  A Alternate pitch  | (from Main only)
 B Bold D Double | H Overprint char  |  N Standard pitch   |^J Help  ^K Block
 S Underscore    | O Non-break space |  C Printing pause   |^Q Quick ^P Print
 X Strikeout     | F Phantom space   |  Y Other ribbon color|^O Onscreen
 V Subscript     | G Phantom rubout  |   --User  Patches--  |Space bar returns
 T Superscript   | RET Overprint line |  Q(1) W(2) E(3) R(4) |you to Main Menu.
 L----!----!----!----!----!----!----!----!----!----!----!--------R
```

**Figure 4**  The print menu.

### The Block Menu

You have already used a number of the commands on the block menu if you have been working the examples in this chapter. Giving the command ^K from the main menu will cause WordStar to place the block menu on your screen. From the block menu you can manipulate blocks of text, whether they are single characters, phrases, or whole files. Figure 5 shows a block menu.

```
^K      B:EXAMPLE   PAGE 1  LINE 1   COL 1        INSERT ON
                    < < <    B L O C K  M E N U    > > >
 -Saving Files-  | -Block Operations- | -File  Operations- |  -Other Menus-
 S Save & resume | B  Begin  K  End   | R  Read  P  Print  |  (from Main only)
 D Save--done    | H  Hide / Display  | O  Copy  E  Rename |  ^J Help  ^K Block
 X Save & exit   | C  Copy   Y  Delete| J  Delete          |  ^Q Quick ^P Print
 Q Abandon file  | V  Move   W  Write | -Disk Operations-  |  ^O Onscreen
 -Place Markers- | N  Column  now OFF |L Change logged disk| Space bar returns
 0-9 Set/hide 0-9|                    |F Directory now OFF | you to Main Menu.
 L----!----!----!----!----!----!----!----!----!----!----!--------R
```

**Figure 5** The block menu.

### The Quick Menu

The quick menu lets you move the cursor faster than one character or word at a time, as we indicated in Section 1.3. In addition, there are commands from the quick menu that allow you to search through a file for a specific character or phrase. You access the quick menu from the main menu by typing ^Q. Figure 6 is what you will see when you do so.

```
^Q      B:EXAMPLE   PAGE 1  LINE 1   COL 1        INSERT ON
                    < < <    Q U I C K  M E N U    > > >
 ---Cursor Movement---  | -Delete- | --Miscellaneous-- | --Other  Menus--
 S left side  D right side |Y line  rt|F Find text in file | (from Main only)
 E top scrn   X bottom scrn|DEL lin lf|A Find & Replace    |^J Help  ^K Block
 R top file   C end file   |          |L Find Misspelling  |^Q Quick ^P Print
 B top block  K end block  |          |Q Repeat command or |^O Onscreen
 0-9 marker   Z up   W down|          |  key  until  space |Space bar returns
 P previous   V last Find or Block    |  bar  or other key |you to Main Menu.
 L----!----!----!----!----!----!----!----!----!----!----!--------R
```

**Figure 6** The quick menu.

172431

## The Help Menu

The help menu is the menu that you call up to find out more about the WordStar commands on the other menus. It is accessed by typing ^J. Essentially, it is a manual on WordStar that you can use when you are learning the different commands. It is shown in Figure 7.

```
^J         B:EXAMPLE  PAGE 1 LINE 1  COL 01           INSERT ON
                 < < <     H E L P   M E N U      > > >
                                              ¦ --Other  Menus--
   H  Display & set the help level ¦ S  Status line    ¦ (from Main only)
   B  Paragraph reform (CONTROL-B) ¦ R  Ruler line      ¦ ^J Help    ^K Block
   F  Flags in right-most column   ¦ M  Margins & Tabs  ¦ ^Q Quick   ^P Print
   D  Dot commands, print controls ¦ P  Place markers   ¦ ^O Onscreen
   I  Index of commands            ¦ V  Moving text     ¦  Space Bar returns
                                   ¦                    ¦  you to Main Menu.
 L----!----!----!----!----!----!----!----!----!----!----!--------R
```

**Figure 7**   The help menu.

# Formatting

Most of the commands covered in this chapter are those found in the on-screen menu. The commands that you access through the on-screen menu are the commands that affect the way in which the characters you type are positioned on the screen. We begin with the commands used to set the left and right margins and the line spacing. In Section 2.2 we look at the another set of commands, called *toggle commands,* that are available through the on-screen menu. In Section 2.3 we take another look at re-forming paragraphs, this time in connection with the commands covered in the first two sections of this chapter. The rest of the chapter contains descriptions of the remaining commands on the on-screen menu.

If you are to the point now where you no longer need to refer to the commands on the main menu, you may want to set the WordStar help level to 2. This way, the main menu will be suppressed, giving you more lines of text on your screen, but the other menus will still show on the screen if you access them. To set the help level to 2, give the command ^JH from the main menu (or just H from the opening menu) and then respond by typing 2 when WordStar prompts you for the new help level.

## 2.1 Setting the Margins and the Line Spacing

When you call up WordStar to begin an editing session, the left margin is automatically set at column 1 and the right margin at column 65. WordStar allows you to change either or both margin settings with the following commands:

| Command | Function |
|---------|----------|
| ^OL | Set left margin |
| ^OR | Set right margin |

**Comments.** Remember, you need to hold down the CONTROL key while you type the first letter of these commands, but it is not necessary to keep the CONTROL key down while you type the second letter. Also, the letters you type can be uppercase or lowercase letters. The margins can be set at any number from 1 to 240. If you set the right margin at a number greater than 80, the newer versions of WordStar will scroll the screen horizontally as you type past column 80. On older versions of WordStar, lines longer than eighty columns are wrapped around onto a second or third line. If a line contains more than eighty characters, you will see a + in the last column on the screen (called the *flag column*). The + indicates that the line continues to the right.

When you press ^OL, WordStar responds with the following message:

```
LEFT MARGIN COLUMN NUMBER (ESCAPE for cursor column)?
```

You respond by typing the number of the column at which you want the left margin set. Then press the RETURN key. If the cursor is in the column at which the left margin is to be set, simply press the ESCAPE key and WordStar will automatically set the left margin at that column. If you are using a version of WordStar installed on the IBM Personal Computer, pressing function key F3 will automatically set the left margin to the column the cursor is in. Likewise, pressing function key F4 will set the right margin at the column in which the cursor lies.

The next command we want to cover is the command to change the line spacing.

| Command | Function |
|---------|----------|
| ^OS | Set line spacing |

**Comments.** When this command is given, WordStar will respond with this message:

```
ENTER space OR NEW LINE SPACING (1-9):
```

You respond by typing a number from 1 to 9 (you don't have to press the RETURN key after doing so), and WordStar will set the line spacing to that number. For instance if you want your text double-spaced on the screen, give the command ^OS 2; to triple-space, type ^OS 3. If you respond by pressing the space bar, the prompt on line spacing disappears from the screen and leaves the line spacing at its current setting.

Here is an example that illustrates how a change in the margin settings and the line spacing affects the way in which your text is placed on the screen.

**Example.** Set the left margin at column 10 ($\wedge$OL 10 RETURN) and the line spacing to 2 ($\wedge$OS 2), and type the paragraph in Figure 1. As you type, notice the movement of the cursor as you type past the right margin. Also, note how the ruler line and status line at the top of the screen have changed.

```
L !----!----!----!----!----!----!----!----!----!--------R
Trigonometry   means   triangle   measure.   The   study   of

trigonometry   arose   out of people's   natural   curiosity

about the relationships that exist between the sides and

angles   in triangles.   I have always been fascinated by

the extent to which trigonometry can be applied to other

fields.
```

**Figure 1** Initial text used to illustrate hyphenation.

Keep this paragraph handy; we will need it again in Section 2.3. If you are going to stop for a while, save it under the file name EXAMPLE2.TXT so we can call it up and use it to practice re-forming paragraphs.

## 2.2 The On-screen Menu Toggle Commands

There are a number of commands on the on-screen menu that are in one of two states: ON or OFF. These commands are referred to as *toggle commands,* or *toggle switches.* Before we explain them, let's look again at the on-screen menu (Figure 2). To get the on-screen menu to appear on your screen, type $\wedge$O.

```
^O      B:LETTER.TXT     PAGE 1 LINE 1     COL 01        INSERT ON
                  < < <  O N S C R E E N   M E N U  > > >
   -Margins & Tabs-  ¦ -Line  Functions-  ¦  --More Toggles--  ¦  -Other  Menus-
   L Set left margin ¦C Center text      ¦J Justify    now ON ¦ (from Main only)
   R Set right margin¦S Set line spacing ¦V Vari-tabs   now ON ¦^J Help  ^K Block
   X Release margins ¦                   ¦H Hyph-help   now ON ¦^Q Quick ^P Print
   I Set  N Clear tab¦    --Toggles--    ¦E Soft hyph now OFF ¦^O Onscreen
   G Paragraph tab   ¦W Wrd wrap  now ON ¦D Prnt disp   now ON ¦Space bar returns
   F Ruler from line ¦T Rlr line  now ON ¦P Pge break   now ON ¦you to Main Menu.
   L----!----!----!----!----!----!----!----!----!----!--------R
```

**Figure 2** The on-screen menu.

The toggle commands, or switches, are listed under the headings *Toggles* and *More Toggles*. For each of these commands, the letter listed first is the letter you press from the on-screen menu to change the commands from their current state. After the letter is a short description of the command, followed by the current setting of the command. For example, the first toggle command, W, is for the word-wrap feature. It is currently ON. To turn it off, you simply press W from the on-screen menu. Word wrap is the WordStar option that takes words that do not fit on the end of a line and puts them on the next line automatically, without requiring you to press the RETURN key.

All the toggle commands work in the same way. If their current state is ON, you can turn them off by typing the letter that is associated with them. Likewise, if they are currently off, you turn them on by typing the letter associated with them.

Here is a list of the rest of the toggle commands with a short explanation of what each of them will do when in the ON state.

| Command | Function |
|---------|----------|
| ^OT | Ruler line on/off |

**Comments.**  The default value for this command is ON. That is, when you purchase a new copy of WordStar, the ruler line toggle command is in the ON state. When the ruler line is on, you see it displayed at the top of the screen or just below any menu that may be showing. When the ruler line is off, it is not displayed, and you have an extra line of text on your screen instead.

| Command | Function |
|---------|----------|
| ^OJ | Justification on/off |

**Comments.**  The default value for the justification is ON. When the justification is on, WordStar places extra spaces, called *soft spaces,* between some of the words on a line so that the last word on the line ends at the right margin. This way, any paragraph you type will be aligned on both the right and left margins. When the justification is off, you get what is called a *ragged* right side on any paragraph you type.

| Command | Function |
|---------|----------|
| ^OV | Variable tabs on/off |

**Comments.**  When the variable tab is on (the default value), you can set the tab stops any place on the ruler line. When off, the tabs are set in fixed postions. For word processing, the variable tabs are almost always kept on.

| Command | Function |
|---------|----------|
| ^OH | Hyphenation help on/off |

**Comments.** The default value for the hyphenation help is ON. In the ON state, WordStar will ask you, during re-forming of paragraphs (^B), if you want to hyphenate long words that appear at the end of a line and extend past the right margin. Many times, hyphenating these words will enhance the way your printed output looks. If the hyphenation help is off, WordStar will not ask you if you want to hyphenate these words. In the next section we include an example that explains in more detail how the hyphenation help works.

| Command | Function |
|---------|----------|
| ^OE | Soft hyphen on/off |

**Comments.** A soft hyphen is a hyphen that will print only when it appears at the end of a line. When the soft-hyphen toggle is off, which is the default value, the only soft hyphens that are placed in your text are the ones that are inserted during re-forming of paragraphs with hyphenation help as explained above. If you turn the soft-hyphen toggle to ON, any hyphen you place in your text will be considered a soft hyphen.

| Command | Function |
|---------|----------|
| ^OD | Print control characters on/off |

**Comments.** When this switch is on, the control characters you insert in your text for things like underlining or bold type will show on the screen. When this switch is off, they will not show on the screen but will still be contained in your file. We will explain this command in more detail in Chapter 3.

| Command | Function |
|---------|----------|
| ^OP | Page break display on/off |

**Comments.** The default value here is ON, meaning that the page break displays will appear on your screen at the end of a page of text. When this switch is off, the page breaks are suppressed.

## 2.3 Re-forming Paragraphs, Hyphenation Help, and Justification

We covered the command for re-forming paragraphs previously in Section 1.3. In this section, we give a more thorough explanation of it. While we explain re-forming paragraphs, we also show some of the details associated with hyphenation help and justification.

| Command | Function |
|---------|----------|
| ^B | Re-form paragraph |

**Comments.** This command can be given at any time during editing. When the command is given, WordStar will re-form all text from the current cursor position to the next carriage return, so that it conforms to the current settings of the left and right margins, the line spacing, and right justification. In addition, if the hyphenation help is on, WordStar will ask you if you want to hyphenate certain words that occur at the end of a line.

**Example.**   Call up file EXAMPLE2.TXT from Section 2.1. Set the left margin at column 10 (^OL 10 RETURN) and the right margin at column 65 (^OR 65 RETURN) if they are not already set at those columns, and then set the line spacing to 1. Now, place the cursor at the beginning of the paragraph, and type ^B (hold the CONTROL key down and press B or b). If the hyphenation help is on, you should see something similar to Figure 3 on your screen.

```
TO HYPHENATE, PRESS -. Before pressing -, you may
    move cursor: ^S=cursor left, ^D=cursor right.
If hyphenation not desired, type ^B.

         L!----!----!----!----!----!----!----!----!----!--------R
         Trigonometry means triangle measure.  The study of trigonometry   arose+
         about the relationships that exist between the sides and
         angles in triangles.   I have always been fascinated  by
         the extent to which trigonometry can be applied to other
         fields.
```

**Figure 3**   Hyphenation help.

Let's put the hyphen between the *g* and the *o* of the word *trigonometry*. Move the cursor one column to the left with ^D, and then press the hyphen key (-). WordStar will hyphenate the word *trigonometry* and then ask if you want to hyphenate the word *angles*. Instead of hyphenating the word *angles,* just give the ^B command again. Now your screen should look like Figure 4.

```
L!----!----!----!----!----!----!----!----!----!--------R
Trigonometry means triangle measure.  The study of trig-
onometry  arose out of people's natural curiosity  about
the relationships  that  exist between  the  sides  and
angles in triangles.   I have always been fascinated by
the extent to which trigonometry can be applied to other
fields.
```

**Figure 4**   Using the soft hyphen.

The hyphen you placed in the word *trigonometry* is a soft hyphen. WordStar will only print it on your printer if it occurs at the end of a line.

Otherwise it is ignored during printing. Now set the left margin back to 1 (^OL 1 RETURN), move the cursor back to the beginning of the para-graph, and give the re-forming paragraphs command again (^B). Note that the hyphen you placed in the word *trigonometry* is still there, even though *trigonometry* is not at the end of a line (some newer versions of WordStar will simply not display the soft hyphen if it is not at the end of a line). Also note that the line containing the soft hyphen extends one column past the right margin. If you move the cursor over the soft hyphen and watch the status line at the top of your screen, you will notice that both the hyphen and the letter next to it are in the same column.

Move the cursor to the hyphen and delete it with ^G.

Now, before we re-form this paragraph again, type ^O and wait until the on-screen menu appears. Look at the on-screen menu and note that the hyphenation help is on. Turn it off by typing H.

Let's re-form our paragraph again. With the margins set at columns 10 and 65, place the cursor at the beginning of the first line of the paragraph and type ^B. Note that, this time, WordStar does not ask you if you want to hyphenate the word *trigonometry*. It simply puts it at the beginning of the next line. With the hyphenation help off, WordStar simply re-forms the paragraph without paying any attention to words that could possibly be hyphenated.

Now let's turn the justification off. Call up the on-screen menu with ^O, and notice that the justification is on. Turn it off by typing J. Next, place the cursor at the beginning of the paragraph, and give the ^B com-mand. The screen should look like Figure 5.

```
L!----!----!----!----!----!----!----!----!----!--------R
Trigonometry means triangle measure.  The study of
trigonometry arose out of people's natural curiosity
about the relationships that exist between the sides and
angles in triangles.  I have always been fascinated by
the extent to which trigonometry can be applied to other
fields.
```

**Figure 5** Justification turned off.

Note that the right side of the paragraph is no longer even; it is ragged. That is because we turned off the justification mode.

## 2.4 Set/Clear Tabs

The tab stops are marked on the ruler line with !'s (exclamation marks). The first tab stop is automatically set by WordStar at column 6. The rest of the tab stops occur every five columns after the first tab stop. These tabs can be deleted, and new ones can be set on the ruler line with the following commands.

| Command | Function |
|---------|----------|
| ^OI | Set tab |
| ^ON | Clear tab |

**Comments.**   Upon receiving the ^OI command, WordStar will respond with the following message:

```
For decimal tab stop enter "#" and a decimal point column
SET TAB AT COLUMN (ESCAPE for cursor column)?
```

If the cursor is currently in the column in which you want a tab set, simply press the ESCAPE key. Otherwise, type in the number of the column you want the tab set in, and then press RETURN. (The top line in the above message is explained in Section 2.5.)

To clear (delete) a previously set tab, give the ^ON command. WordStar will respond with this message:

```
CLEAR TAB AT COL (ESCAPE for cursor col; A for all)?
```

Pressing the ESCAPE key will delete any tab in the same column as the cursor. Pressing A will clear the ruler line of all tab stops. Typing a column number followed by RETURN will delete the tab at that column.

## 2.5  Decimal Tabs

There are times when WordStar is so helpful in simplifying complicated procedures that you wonder how they thought of it. The idea of decimal tab stops is one such idea.

Let's illustrate the idea of decimal tabs with an example.

**Example.**  Call up WordStar, and create a file with the file name EXAMPLE3.TXT. Type the following paragraph as an introduction.

```
Decimal  tabs are used to align the decimal points when  entering
columns  of  numbers.   On  the ruler  line,  a  decimal  tab  is
designated  by  the  symbol #.   If you use the tab key  on  your
terminal to stop at a decimal tab,  the next character you ·enter
will  be  placed to the left of the cursor.   This will  continue
until you hit the space bar, the TAB key, or a period.
```

Now, clear all tab stops with the ^ON A command. Set a regular tab stop at column 10 (^OI 10 RETURN). Next, set decimal tab stops in columns 30 and 45, by giving the command ^OI and responding with #30 RETURN, followed by another ^OI and then #40 RETURN. (If the cursor is in the column in which you want a decimal tab set, just type # and press ESCAPE). Look at the ruler line; it should look like this:

```
L--------!--------------------#--------------#--------------------R
```

Next, below the introductory paragraph you have just entered, type in the following table. Use the space bar to begin the headings in columns 11, 26, and 41. After that use the TAB key to enter each month and the numbers that follow. Notice how WordStar automatically lines up the decimal points. Note also what happens to the status line at the top of the screen when you tab over to a decimal tab.

```
First Quarter Report
          Month        Income        Expenses
          January      $6,491.58     $263.45
          February        29.03      789.54
          March          423.44        3.90
          April           27.46       98.13
```

The finished product should look like Figure 6.

```
L--------!--------------------#--------------#--------------------R
Decimal  tabs are used to align the decimal points when  entering
columns  of  numbers.   On  the  ruler line,  a  decimal  tab  is
designated  by  the symbol #.   If you use the tab  key  on  your
terminal  to stop at a decimal tab,  the next character you enter
will  be placed to the left of the cursor.   This  will  continue
until you hit the space bar, the tab key, or a period.

First Quarter Report

          Month        Income        Expenses
          January      $6,491.58     $263.45
          February        29.03      789.54
          March          423.44        3.90
          April           27.46       98.13
```

**Figure 6**  Text with decimal tabs.

## 2.6 Creating and Saving a New Ruler Line

When I first started using WordStar to create tables with columns of numbers in them, I spent a lot more time moving the cursor to the different columns than I needed to. If I had two tables with the same format, but appearing on different pages, I kept moving back and forth between the two tables because I would forget which columns I had set the tab stops in. Then I discovered that WordStar allows you to create a new ruler line and to save it in your document.

To create your own ruler line, begin by typing a capital L where you want the left margin set. Then type any combination of hyphens, exclamation marks (!), and #'s. Type a capital R in the last column of your ruler line. To tell WordStar that you want this line to become the ruler line, you use the command explained below.

| Command | Function |
|---------|----------|
| ^OF | Ruler from current line |

**Comments.** The cursor must be on the new ruler line when this command is given. When the new ruler line is created, make sure that all the hyphens you use are hard hyphens. (Look at the ^O menu to see that "E soft hyph on" is in OFF).

Once you have created a new ruler line, you may want to save it so that the next time you edit the document in which it occurs you won't have to create it again. The idea is to save it in the document so that you can see it on the screen, but in such a way that WordStar will ignore it when printing and not count it in the line number count. To do this, move the cursor to column 1 of the new ruler line and, with the INSERT ON, type two periods. WordStar will then treat this line as a comment line. The next time you call up this document and find that you want to edit the table or text created under this ruler line, simply delete the two periods you typed and give the ^OF command. Then reinsert the two periods and you are all set.

Another way to save the new ruler line, so that WordStar will ignore it in the line count and while printing, is to overprint it on a comment line. To do this, begin your comment line with two periods followed by any message you want to place on that line. End the line by typing ^P followed by RETURN. WordStar will then place a hyphen in the flag column of that line. The hyphen in the flag column indicates that the next line is to be overprinted on the comment line you just typed. Now type in your ruler line.

WordStar now ignores both lines while printing and in the line count. To change to this ruler line, you simply place the cursor anywhere on it and give the ^OF command. With this method of placing a new ruler line in your file, there is no need to delete the leading periods.

## 2.7 Temporary Indentation and Margin Release

It is not uncommon, when creating documents, to have a paragraph or two that are indented from the left margin. WordStar allows you to format text in this manner by temporarily resetting the left margin to any one of the tab stops.

| Command | Function |
|---------|----------|
| ^OG | Reset left margin to next tab stop |

**Comments.** Giving the ^OG command once will reset the left margin to the first tab stop. The left margin will remain set at that tab stop until you hit the RETURN key or back the cursor up to a point previous to the point at which you gave the command. If you want to temporarily set the left margin at the second tab stop, give the ^OG command twice. Give the command three times, and WordStar will temporarily set the left margin at the third tab stop.

**Example.** Type the text in Figure 7. The margins should be set at columns 1 and 65, the first tab stop at column 6. To indent the material that follows the number 1, type the 1 and the period, and then give the ^OG command and continue typing.

```
L----!----!----!----!----!----!----!----!----!----!----!--------R
      There  are two main relationships we want to consider   while
investigating the properties of matter, they are as follows:

1.   Under what conditions can we expect the physical  properties
     to  change.   Generally speaking,  we want to know if it  is
     possible  to change the way matter looks,  without  changing
     its chemical composition.

2.   What  conditions  will  give rise to a  chemical  change  in
     matter,  and  how  will we be able to tell that  a  chemical
     change has taken place.
```

**Figure 7** Example of temporary indentation and margin release.

If your terminal is capable of highlighting or reverse video, notice what happens to the ruler line when you give the ^OG command: the characters preceding the tab stop are highlighted or displayed in reverse video.

Besides allowing us to change the left margin temporarily, WordStar is also capable of temporarily releasing both margins.

| Command | Function |
|---------|----------|
| ^OX | Release margins |

**Comments.**   When this command is given, the phrase *MAR REL* will appear at the top of the screen on the status line. The margins will stay released until you type ^OX again or move the cursor back between the margins. WordStar will place a plus sign in the last column of the lines that go beyond the right side of the screen. This command is useful if you want to put notes or headings in the left or right margin next to the text you have typed.

## 2.8  Putting It All Together

To enter the following page of text, you will have to use most of the commands covered in this chapter. You can use a decimal tab to align the numbers on their decimal points, and you can use the temporary indent command, ^OG, on those paragraphs that are indented. To begin, the margins, tabs, and line spacing should be set to the default values.

L----!----!----!----!----!---#!----!----!----!----!----!--------R
Section One:  Adding Decimal Fractions

To  add  two  or more decimal  fractions,  we  first  write  them

vertically, one under the other, with the decimal points aligned.

Then  we  add in columns as we would if we were adding  integers.

The  decimal  point in the answer is placed  directly  below  the

decimal points in the problem.

Example 1  Add:  2.543 + 136.08 + 13.3

> Solution   We begin by writing the numbers one under another
> with  the  decimal points aligned.   Then we add in  columns,
> and place the decimal point in the answer directly below the
> decimal point in the numbers.

$$
\begin{array}{r}
2.543 \\
136.08 \\
13.3 \\
\hline
151.923
\end{array}
$$

> Notice that we could fill in zeros to the right of the  last
> two digits in 136.08 and 13.3 to justify adding in columns.

$$
\begin{array}{r}
2.543 \\
136.080 \\
13.300 \\
\hline
151.923
\end{array}
$$

# Chapter

# 3

# Printing Functions

We begin this chapter with a look at the commands that cause WordStar to print a file. Since there are a number of options available with these commands, we discuss them also. After the commands to print a file have been covered, we list the commands that are used to place control characters into a file in order to take advantage of some of the special printing features of most printers.

## 3.1 Printing a File

Once a file has been created with WordStar, it can be printed from the opening menu by pressing P or during editing by pressing ∧KP.

| Command from opening menu | Function |
|:-:|:-:|
| P | Print a file |

**Comments.** After you give this command, WordStar will ask you for the name of the file you would like to print. You respond with the file name of the file to be printed, preceding it with the letter of the drive on which it resides, and a colon, if the file is not on the disk currently in use. For example, if you want to print the file EXAMPLE2.TXT and it is on drive B, and you are currently working on drive A, you type B:EXAMPLE2.TXT followed by RETURN. If WordStar cannot find the file you have specified, you will see this message displayed on the screen:

```
File "B:EXAMPLE2.TXT" not found
```

If you have made a mistake in the spelling of the file name or referenced the wrong drive, simply type in the correct information and press RETURN again. Once you have given WordStar the correct name of the file you want to print, you will be asked a number of questions about how you want the file to be printed. We will cover the responses to these questions after we have given you a chance to print one of the files you created earlier.

**Example.**   Print the file EXAMPLE1.TXT or EXAMPLE2.TXT that you created in Chapters 1 and 2. To do so, type P from the opening (or no-file) menu, give the file name when WordStar asks for it, and then press RETURN in response to each of the questions WordStar asks.

### Options Available during Printing

Once WordStar has found the file to be printed, it will ask you a number of questions about the manner in which to print the file. Each question has a default answer that can be given by simply pressing the RETURN key in response to the question. (You can bypass the questions at any point after you give the name of the file to be printed by simply pressing the ESCAPE key on your keyboard.)

In the remainder of this section we cover all the possible responses to the questions WordStar asks about how you want your file printed. In most cases, especially if you are just beginning to use WordStar, you will use the default values for these options. Therefore, you may want to skip this section and read through the rest of the chapter before coming back to read about the printing options.

Here is the first question that WordStar asks after you have supplied the name of the file you want to print.

```
DISK FILE OUTPUT (Y/N):
```

The (Y/N) expression stands for *yes* or *no*. A no response is the default response and is initiated by typing N (again, it doesn't have to be a capital N) or RETURN or any other letter except Y, y, or ^Y. If you type Y for yes, WordStar will respond with

```
OUTPUT FILE NAME?
```

You then give the drive letter, colon, and a file name. During printing, WordStar will place a print image of the file you named originally on the disk and file it under this new name. This print image will be a copy of your original file with all the dot commands (explained later on in Chapter 5) and control characters expanded. Why would you want to do this? In some cases you may have so many dot commands and control characters embedded in your file that you will have a difficult time seeing how the file will look when printed. You can use this option to print that file to a disk under a different file name, so that you can call the file up and see what it looks like, and maybe do some additional editing, before you print it.

After a yes or no response to the DISK FILE OUTPUT question, WordStar will ask:

START AT PAGE NUMBER (RETURN for beginning)?

If you want WordStar to print your file starting at page 1, simply press RETURN or 1. If you want to begin printing at some other page, enter that page number and press RETURN. If you have used the dot command .PN # (to be fully explained in Section 5.1), you will have to adjust your response to this question accordingly. If you want to begin printing at the third page of a file that begins with a .PG 5 command, you must respond to this question by pressing 8 and then RETURN.

The next question from WordStar is

STOP AFTER PAGE NUMBER (RETURN for end)?

The responses here are similar to the response to the preceding question, except that you are now referencing the last page to be printed.

USE FORM FEEDS (Y/N)

The default response for this question is N, and is the proper response for most letter-quality printers and dot-matrix printers that have the "form feed" option. On dot-matrix printers without the form feed option, the printer will move the paper up one line for each blank line at the end of the page. (For example, if page 1 has only ten lines on it, with the last forty-five lines blank, WordStar will send forty-five line feeds to the printer to get to the top of the next page.) You can save time in printing with this type of dot-matrix printer by responding yes to this question.

SUPPRESS PAGE FORMATTING (Y/N):

Responding yes to this question will cause WordStar to print the dot commands in the file but not interpret them. Most other print control characters, like ^B, will be interpreted and have their normal effect during printing. Why would you want to respond yes to this question? One reason could be that you have a file with many dot commands embedded throughout. You could use a yes response here to get a printed copy of that file and its dot commands so that you could proofread it. Another situation in which a yes response is appropriate is when printing a file created with a yes response to the first question, "DISK FILE OUT-PUT?" A file of this type has already been formatted on the disk.

PAUSE FOR PAPER CHANGE BETWEEN PAGES (Y/N):

The default for this question is no. A yes response here will cause the printer to pause at the end of each page so that a new piece of paper can be put in. To resume printing, press P on the keyboard.

READY PRINTER, PRESS RETURN:

When you have readied your printer, press RETURN or any other key and printing will begin.

**Note.** You can bypass any or all of the above questions by pressing the ESCAPE key. For instance, if you want only the default responses to all questions, simply press ESCAPE after giving the name of the file to be printed and WordStar will begin printing without asking any questions. If you want to begin printing on page 5, you can answer the first two questions and then press ESCAPE to bypass the remaining questions.

Once printing has begun, WordStar will return to the opening menu while printing is in progress. Notice that Stop Print is highlighted on the opening menu in place of Print a File. Pressing P during printing will stop the printer and produce the following message on the screen.

TYPE "Y" TO ABANDON PRINT, "N" TO RESUME, ^U TO HOLD:

If you respond to this message by typing Y, printing will be abandoned and WordStar will return to the opening menu. Typing N will cause WordStar to continue printing. Typing ^U will return WordStar to the opening menu, where you can call up a file to edit or anything else you usually do from the opening menu.

## 3.2 Boldface and Doublestrike

The commands we cover in this section, and the rest of the chapter, are the commands found on the print menu. You can preview these commands by typing ^P from the main menu. The commands on the print menu allow you to insert messages to your printer into your files. With these commands, you can tell your printer to print characters in boldface, underline characters, doublestrike characters, and overstrike characters, among other things. In addition, you can tell your printer to do a number of these things simultaneously.

Let's begin by looking at how WordStar tells your printer to print in boldface. A character printed in boldface is darker and a little wider than characters printed in the normal print mode. WordStar achieves this by printing the character as it normally would and then printing it a second time $\frac{1}{120}$ of an inch to the right, if you are using a letter-quality printer. With a dot-matrix printer, boldface is printed by striking each character three times. The command that sends these instructions to the printer is embedded in the text, before and after the characters that are to be printed in boldface.

| Command | Function |
|---------|----------|
| ^PB | Begin/end boldface |

**Comments.**  To give this command, depress the CONTROL key and type P while the CONTROL key is held down. Then type B. (Neither the P or B have to be capitals.) If more than a second goes by between the time you type the P and the B, the print menu will come on the screen. Giving this command will cause WordStar to insert a ^B at the cursor position. When you print the file, the ^B will instruct your printer to begin boldface printing. The printer will continue to print in boldface until it encounters another ^B.

**Note.**  The two spaces taken up by ^B on the screen are not counted in the line length. If your margins are set so that you have sixty-five characters per line, and one complete line of text contains a ^B, then you will see sixty-seven characters on that line when it is displayed on the screen. If the justification is on, it may look like the lines containing control characters are running over the right margin. They are not, because, during printing, WordStar will not print the ^B's.

**Example.**  Type the following paragraph, then save it with ^KS, and print it with ^KP. (Remember, the ^B's are obtained by typing ^PB.)

```
L----!----!----!----!----!----!----!----!----!----!----!--------R
     This line contains ^Bboldface type^B.  It is obtained by typing
P and then B with the control key depressed.
```

When your file is printed, this will print as:

```
     This line contains boldface type.   It is obtained by typing
   P and then B with the control key depressed.
```

A command that is similar to the boldface command is the doublestrike command. It is also used to emphasize type.

| Command | Function |
|---------|----------|
| ^PD | Begin/end doublestrike |

**Comments.** This command will place a ^D in your text at the cursor position. This causes your printer to strike each character following the ^D twice. The effect is darker type, but not as dark as boldface type. The next ^D command will return the printer to single strike mode.

## 3.3 Underline, Strikeout, and Overprint

In addition to boldface and doublestrike, WordStar will accommodate a number of other print commands. The instructions for these commands are similar to those that are used to produce boldface type.

| Command | Function |
|---------|----------|
| ^PS | Begin/end underline |

**Comments.** This command will insert ^S into your text, which will cause the printer to begin underlining characters. All characters will be underlined until the next ^S is encountered. Also, only nonblank spaces are underlined.

| Command | Function |
|---------|----------|
| ^PX | Begin/end strikeout |

**Comments.** With this command, WordStar will overprint all nonblank characters between two ^X's with a hyphen (-). This command is very useful for legal documents and things of that nature.

The example that follows illustrates the print control characters we have covered so far in this chapter.

**Example.**  Type the following paragraph. (Remember, ^B is obtained by typing P with the CONTROL key depressed, and then typing B.)

```
L----!----!----!----!----!----!----!----!----!----!----!--------R
        WordStar  will  print  ^Bboldface type^B and  ^Ddoublestrike  type^D  by
typing   each   character  more  than  once.    It can  also  ^Sunderline
characters^S  and  ^Xoverstrike them^X with hyphens.   WordStar is  also
capable  of  doing  two  or  more of these print features at the same
time.   For  example,  we  could  ^B^Sunderline our boldface type^S^B if  we
choose.  Or,  we  could  ^B^S^Xstrike it out^B^S^X at the same time.
```

When printed, this paragraph will look like this:

```
        WordStar will print **boldface type** and doublestrike type by
typing each character more than once.   It can also underline
characters and overstrike them with hyphens.  WordStar is also
capable of doing two or more of these print features at the same
time.  For example, we could underline our boldface type if we
choose.  Or, we could strike it out at the same time.
```

In some situations, you may prefer to strikeout a string of characters with a slash (/) or x's. WordStar allows you to do this one line at a time.

| Command | Function |
|---------|----------|
| ^P RETURN | Overstrike with next line |

**Comments.**  The ^P RETURN must be placed after the last character on the line you want to overprint. The next line contains the overprint characters. When this command is given, WordStar will put a hyphen (-) on the screen in the last column (flag column) of the line to be overprinted. Note that this command may not work on some printers, especially dot-matrix printers.

**Example.**  Type the following three lines, save them with ^KS, and then print them with ^KP.

```
L----!----!----!----!----!----!----!----!----!----!----!--------R
The closing costs will be paid by the seller.^P RETURN
/////////////////////////////////////////////////
The closing costs will be paid by the buyer.
```

When printed, the three lines above will print as the following two lines.

```
T̸h̸e̸/̸c̸l̸o̸s̸i̸n̸g̸/̸c̸o̸s̸t̸s̸/̸w̸i̸l̸l̸/̸b̸e̸/̸p̸a̸i̸d̸/̸b̸y̸/̸t̸h̸e̸/̸s̸e̸l̸l̸e̸r̸.
The closing costs will be paid by the buyer.
```

Finally, WordStar contains a command that will overstrike one character at a time.

| Command | Function |
|---------|----------|
| ^PH | Overstrike next character |

**Comments.** Typing this command will cause ^H to be embedded in your text at the cursor position. This causes the printer to back up one space and print the next character. The effect is that the character that occurs before the ^H is overprinted with the character that follows the ^H. The ^H and the character that follows it are not counted as characters in the line count. Because of this, lines containing ^H may extend past the right margin on your screen.

**Example.** Type and then print the following three sentences.

```
L----!----!----!----!----!----!----!----!----!----!----!--------R
    In  Spanish, the name Jose^H` has an accent mark over the last
letter.
    In trigonometry, the cosine of angle 0^H- (theta) is
abbreviated cos 0^H-.
    In computer science, it is important to distinguish the
letter 0 from the number 0^H/.
```

When printed, these sentences should look like this:

```
        In Spanish, the name Josè has an accent mark over the last
letter.
        In trigonometry, the cosine of angle θ (theta) is
abbreviated cos θ.
        In computer science, it is important to distinguish the
letter O from the number Ø.
```

## 3.4  Nonbreak Space

There are times when it is important that characters separated by a space occur on the same line. For example, in chemistry, the equation pH = 3.7 will usually look better, and be easier to read, if all the characters appear on the same line. If this equation were to occur toward the end of a line, however, it may be possible that the word wrap feature of WordStar would break it before or after the equal sign. To take care of this potential problem, WordStar has a feature, accessed through the P menu, called nonbreak space.

| Command | Function |
|---------|----------|
| ^PO | Nonbreak space |

**Comments.**  Typing this command will cause ^O to occur at the cursor position. The function of the ^O is to keep the preceding string of nonblank characters and the succeeding string of nonblank characters together. The ^O will be counted as one space by WordStar.

**Example.**  With the left margin set at 1 and the right margin set at 65, type the following sentence.

```
L----!----!----!----!----!----!----!----!----!----!----!--------R
      If your line length is set at 65 characters, and you type pH
= 3.7,  part of it will occur on one line and part on the  other,
unless  you  replace the spaces around the = sign with  non-break
spaces.
```

Now go back and delete the spaces before and after the equal sign with ^G, and then replace then with ^PO. Notice what happens if you move the cursor to the beginning of the sentence and then re-form it with ∧B. The result will look like this.

```
L----!----!----!----!----!----!----!----!----!----!----!--------R
     If  your line length is set at 65 characters,  and you  type
pH^O=^O3.7,  part  of  it  will occur on one line and part  on  the
other,  unless you replace the spaces around the = sign with non-
break spaces.
```

## 3.5 Other Print Commands

In this section we list the remaining print commands that can be accessed through the P menu. The first of these commands allows you to stop your printer in order to change type wheels or thimbles in the middle of a page or line.

| Command | Function |
|---------|----------|
| ∧PC | Print pause |

**Comments.** This command causes a ∧C to be placed in the text at the cursor position. Upon receipt of ∧C, the printer will stop printing and the terminal will display:

PRINT PAUSED

on the status line. To start printing, simply press P on the keyboard.

**Note.** With some printers, the ∧C will not stop printing in the middle of a line. In these cases, place your ∧C at the beginning of a blank line and the printer will stop between lines.

| Command | Function |
|---------|----------|
| ∧PY | Change ribbon color |

**Comments.** If your printer is equipped with a two-color ribbon option, placing ∧Y in your text will cause the printer to begin printing in the second color. The next ∧Y will return printing to the original color.

| Command | Function |
|---------|----------|
| ∧PA | Select alternate pitch |
| ∧PN | Select normal pitch |

**Comments.**  These commands were intended to be used with a letter-quality printer. When your letter-quality printer encounters ^A in your file, it will begin printing twelve characters per inch (twelve-pitch type). The printer will continue printing twelve character per inch until it encounters ^N, at which time it will return to ten characters per inch, which is the default value.

**Note.**  Both the normal pitch and alternate pitch can be changed from the default values of ten and twelve. An example of this is given in Section 5.3. Note also that, since these commands will probably not have any effect on a dot-matrix printer, it may be wise to set up some other function for these commands when you install WordStar for such a printer.

# 4

# Equations

In this chapter we consider the procedures used to enter and format equations. The commands that we introduce in this chapter are found on the on-screen (^O) menu or the print (^P) menu. In the last section of the chapter we introduce the first of our dot commands. The rest of the dot commands are explained in Chapter 5.

We begin this chapter by looking at some simple equations that are to be displayed in the center of the printed page. After that, we consider equations that contain superscripts (exponents) and subscripts. If you are using a dot-matrix printer, you may find that a number of the commands in this chapter do not work in the same way on your printer as they do in the examples here. Most of the commands in this chapter are intended for use with a letter-quality printer. It is possible to install many dot-matrix printers so that they can take better advantage of the commands in this chapter. If you are using a dot-matrix printer, you may want to read through the appendix on installing your printer and then come back to this chapter. In any case, reading through this chapter, and trying the examples on your printer, will show you what your printer can and cannot do.

## 4.1 Centering Equations and Aligning Equal Signs

When a series of equations are to be typed one below another in a technical manuscript, the usual format is to center the longest equation and then align the equal signs in the other equations with the equal sign in the centered equation. If a phrase or short sentence appears to the right of any of the equations, for the purpose of centering it is considered to be part of the equation.

To center a line of text, we first type in the line and then use the following command.

| Command | Function |
|---------|----------|
| ^OC | Center a line |

**Comments.**  This command is used after the line to be centered has been typed. The cursor must appear on the line to be centered, but it can be in any column on that line. For purposes of centering, any control characters in the line to be centered and spaces before or after the line are ignored.

**Example.**  Type the following two lines and then center each one.

```
L----!----!----!----!----!----!----!----!----!----!----!--------R
                    This is a displayed equation.

                       3x - 4 = -2x + 1
```

To display a series of equations so that the longest line is centered and the equal signs in the other equations are aligned with the equal sign in the longest line, we first type each equation on a separate line. Then we move the cursor to the longest line and center it using ^OC. Finally, with the INSERT ON, we put the cursor at the beginning of each of the other lines and use the TAB key and space bar to insert spaces before the first character of each equation until the equal signs are aligned. (If you move an equation too far to the right, you can move the cursor back a few spaces and then delete those spaces with ^G.)

**Example.**  Type the following five lines beginning in column 1. Then center the longest line and insert spaces in front of the other equations to align the equal signs.

```
L----!----!----!----!----!----!----!----!----!----!----!--------R
This is a series of displayed equations centered on the page.

3x - 4 = -2x + 1

5x - 4 = 1

5x = 5

x = 1
```

The finished product should look like this:

```
L----!----!----!----!----!----!----!----!----!----!----!--------R
This is a series of displayed equations centered on the page.
                        3x - 4 = -2x + 1

                        5x - 4 = 1

                            5x = 5

                             x = 1
```

Many times, a series of equations that are to be displayed on the page will be such that a number of the equations do not have any characters to the left of the equal sign. In these situations we can save time by erasing the tabs on the ruler line and then setting a tab on the column that is to contain the equal sign.

**Example.** Type the following lines, centering the first two of them. Then erase all tab stops using ^ON A RETURN, and set a new tab at the column containing the equal sign in the first equation. On all the lines that follow, use the TAB key to put the cursor in that column, and then begin typing.

```
L----!----!----!----!----!----!----!----!----!----!----!--------R
More displayed equations

2 + 3(9 - 4) - 6 = 2 + 3(5) - 6

= 2 + 15 - 6

= 17 - 6

= 11
```

The result will look like this:

```
L-------------------------------!----------------------------R
More displayed equations
                2 + 3(9 - 4) - 6 = 2 + 3(5) - 6
                                = 2 + 15 - 6
                                = 17 - 6
                                = 11
```

## 4.2 Superscripts I (Exponents) and Hiding Control Characters

Many expressions found in science and mathematics require the use of *superscripted characters*. A superscripted character is a character that will be printed a half-line above the line on which the surrounding characters are typed. For example, the 2 in $5x^2$ is superscripted, as is the expression *log* x in $10^{\log x}$. To obtain superscripts we use the following command.

| Command | Function |
|---------|----------|
| ^PT | Begin/end superscript |

**Comments.** We type ^P followed by T before and after the character or characters to be superscripted. The screen will display only ^T. On most letter-quality printers, the first ^T instructs the printer to roll the paper down a half line, while the second ^T instructs the printer to return the paper to its original position. If a series of consecutive characters are to be superscripted, we need only one ^T before the first character and one ^T after the last character. It is not necessary to place a ^T before and after each character to be superscripted. The ^T's that appear on the screen will not appear on the printout. Also note that a line on your screen containing ^T may end past the right margin.

**Note on Dot-Matrix Printers.** If you are using a dot-matrix printer, you may find that your printer will ignore a ^T if your text is single spaced. Also, you may find that your printer places superscripts up a whole line instead of a half line. Neither of these characteristics is desirable if you are going to be printing files that contain mathematical text. Many times you can get around these problems by doing a customized installation of your printer using the WordStar installation program. For instance, my Epson FX-80 printer prints superscripts in the same way that my letter-quality printer does, because I have installed it that way.

Figure 1 shows the screen display of some text that contains a number of superscripted characters. Figure 2 is the corresponding hard copy of the screen display in Figure 1, printed on a letter-quality printer in twelve pitch type. Note the ^A command at the beginning of the file. It instructs a letter-quality printer to print twelve characters per inch. You need this command if you are using a twelve-pitch thimble, or twelve-pitch daisy wheel, on a letter-quality printer. It will be ignored or have a different function if you are using a dot-matrix printer.

```
L----!----!----!----!----!----!----!----!----!----!--------R
^A^BExample 1^B  Solve x^T4^T - x^T3^T - 6x^T2^T = 0 for x.

      ^BSolution^B   To solve the equation for x we begin by factoring
      the  left side.   Then we set each of the factors to  0  and
      solve the resulting equations.

                    x^T4^T - x^T3^T - 6x^T2^T = 0

                    x^T2^T(x^T2^T - x - 6) = 0

                    x^T2^T(x - 3)(x + 2) = 0

              x^T2^T = 0  or  x - 3 = 0  or x + 2 = 0

              x = 0           x = 3          x = -2
```

**Figure 1**  Superscripted characters.

**Example 1**  Solve $x^4 - x^3 - 6x^2 = 0$ for x.

**Solution**  To solve the equation for x we begin by factoring the left side.   Then we set each of the factors to 0 and solve the resulting equations.

$$x^4 - x^3 - 6x^2 = 0$$

$$x^2(x^2 - x - 6) = 0$$

$$x^2(x - 3)(x + 2) = 0$$

$$x^2 = 0 \quad \text{or} \quad x - 3 = 0 \quad \text{or} \quad x + 2 = 0$$

$$x = 0 \qquad x = 3 \qquad x = -2$$

**Figure 2**  Print sample of Figure 1 from an NEC Spinwriter with twelve-pitch thimble.

Don't be discouraged if you have tried the example above on your dot-matrix printer and have found that the print sample does not look as nice as you would like. Figure 3 shows the printout of Figure 1 again, but this time using an Epson FX-80 printer installed so that superscripts are printed by rolling the paper down a half line. To install your dot-matrix printer so that it will produce a printed page like the one in Figure 3, your printer must be capable of rolling the paper up and down a half line.

---

Example 1    Solve $x^4 - x^3 - 6x^2 = 0$ for x.

Solution    To solve the equation for x we begin by factoring the left side.    Then we set each of the factors to 0 and solve the resulting equations.

$$x^4 - x^3 - 6x^2 = 0$$

$$x^2(x^2 - x - 6) = 0$$

$$x^2(x - 3)(x + 2) = 0$$

$$x^2 = 0 \quad \text{or} \quad x - 3 = 0 \quad \text{or} \quad x + 2 = 0$$

$$x = 0 \qquad\qquad x = 3 \qquad\qquad x = -2$$

---

**Figure 3**  Print sample of Figure 1 from an Epson FX-80 printer.

If you tried the previous example, you probably noticed that the ^T's in Figure 1 make it difficult to align the equal signs in the equations. We can take care of this problem by hiding the control characters. Here is the command that does so.

| **Command** | **Function** |
|:-----------:|:------------:|
| ^OD | Hide/display control characters |

**Comments.**  Giving this command will cause WordStar to hide the control characters in your file if they are currently displayed, and display them if they are currently hidden. The command has no affect on the position of the control characters in your file. That is, when you hide the control characters, they are still part of your file, even though they are not showing on your screen.

Figure 4 shows the screen display from Figure 1 again, but this time with the ^OD command in effect.

```
L----!----!----!----!----!----!----!----!----!----!----!--------R
Example 1   Solve x4 - x3 - 6x2 = 0 for x.
```

Solution   To solve the equation for x we begin by factoring
the  left side.    Then we set each of the factors to  0  and
solve the resulting equations.

$$x4 - x3 - 6x2 = 0$$

$$x2(x2 - x - 6) = 0$$

$$x2(x - 3)(x + 2) = 0$$

$$x2 = 0 \quad \text{or} \quad x - 3 = 0 \quad \text{or} \quad x + 2 = 0$$

$$x = 0 \qquad\qquad x = 3 \qquad\qquad x = -2$$

**Figure 4**  Employing the $\wedge$OD command.

**Shortcuts.** Entering text that contains numerous superscripts can become very time consuming, simply because of how often you would have to type $\wedge$PT. If your terminal is equipped with programmable function keys, programming one of these keys to output $\wedge$PT will cut down your typing time considerably. If the manuscript contains numerous repetitions of the same superscripted character, the WordStar *Find and Replace Command* can save you even more time (see Section 7.2).

## 4.3 Superscripts II: Special Print Thimbles and Character Sets

In this section we look at the the way in which the special character sets, available on some printers, can be used to produce superscripts and subscripts. Since letter-quality printers access special characters in a different manner than dot-matrix printers do, we treat each of them separately.

### Letter-Quality Printers

There is a wide variety of print thimbles or daisy wheels available with most letter-quality printers. The *Tech Math/Times Roman* and *Scientific/Times Roman* thimbles for the NEC Spinwriter printers contain special exponent symbols in addition to the normal American Standard Code for Information Interchange (ASCII) characters. This gives us an alternative to typing exponents with superscripts. We can access the exponents on these thimbles with the following command.

| Command | Function |
|---------|----------|
| ^PQ | Begin new font |
| ^PW | Return to normal font |

**Comments.** When ^PQ is in effect, many of the keys on the keyboard will print special characters and symbols during printing. For exponents, an uppercase W will print as the exponent 2 when enclosed by ^Q and ^W. To print the exponent 3, enclose an uppercase E between ^Q and ^W. The exponents 4 through 9 and 0 are accessed with the rest of the upper-case letters, in sequence, on the top row of letters on the keyboard. Thus each of the following characters will print as the exponents listed below them when enclosed by ^Q^W.

```
Q W E R T Y U I O P
1 2 3 4 5 6 7 8 9 0
```

Figure 5 shows the screen display for the screen in Figure 1 with the exponents entered using the ^PQ and ^PW commands. Figure 6 is the hard copy of that screen display.

```
L----!----!----!----!----!----!----!----!----!----!----!--------R
^A^BExample 1^B  Solve x^QR^W - x^QE^W - 6x^QW^W = 0 for x.

     ^BSolution^B   To solve the equation for x we begin by factoring
     the  left  side.    Then we set each of the factors to  0   and
     solve the resulting equations.

                   x^QR^W - x^QE^W - 6x^QW^W = 0

                   x^QW^W(x^QW^W - x - 6) = 0

                   x^QW^W(x - 3)(x + 2) = 0

             x^QW^W = 0   or   x - 3 = 0   or x + 2 = 0

              x = 0            x = 3           x = -2
```

**Figure 5**  Employing the ^PQ and ^PW commands.

**Example 1**   Solve $x^4 - x^3 - 6x^2 = 0$ for x.

**Solution**   To solve the equation for x we begin by factoring the left side. Then we set each of the factors to 0 and solve the resulting equations.

$$x^4 - x^3 - 6x^2 = 0$$

$$x^2(x^2 - x - 6) = 0$$

$$x^2(x - 3)(x + 2) = 0$$

$$x^2 = 0 \quad \text{or} \quad x - 3 = 0 \quad \text{or} \quad x + 2 = 0$$

$$x = 0 \qquad\qquad x = 3 \qquad\qquad x = -2$$

**Figure 6**   Print sample of Figure 5 from an NEC Spinwriter with Tech Math/Times Roman thimble.

## Dot-Matrix Printers

Many dot-matrix printers have an alternate character set built into them. The Epson FX-80 has a complete set of characters that can be used as superscripts. They are smaller than the normal characters and are raised up about a half a line. I have installed my FX-80 so the $\wedge$PQ command instructs the printer to begin printing these characters, while the $\wedge$PW commands returns the printer to its normal print mode. Figure 7 shows the screen in Figure 1 again with $\wedge$PQ before the characters to be superscripted and $\wedge$PW after them. Figure 8 shows how the screen in Figure 7 looks when printed on the Epson.

```
L----!----!----!----!----!----!----!----!----!----!----!--------R
^BExample 1^B  Solve x^Q4^W - x^Q3^W - 6x^Q2^W = 0 for x.

        ^BSolution^B   To solve the equation for x we begin by factoring
        the left side.    Then we set each of the factors to  0  and
        solve the resulting equations.

                   x^Q4^W - x^Q3^W - 6x^Q2^W = 0

                   x^Q2^W(x^Q2^W - x - 6) = 0

                   x^Q2^W(x - 3)(x + 2) = 0

             x^Q2^W = 0  or  x - 3 = 0  or  x + 2 = 0

               x = 0        x = 3        x = -2
```

**Figure 7**   Employing the $\wedge$PQ and $\wedge$PW commands for a letter-quality printer.

Example 1   Solve $x^4 - x^3 - 6x^2 = 0$ for x.

Solution   To solve the equation for x we begin by factoring the left side.   Then we set each of the factors to 0 and solve the resulting equations.

$$x^4 - x^3 - 6x^2 = 0$$

$$x^2(x^2 - x - 6) = 0$$

$$x^2(x - 3)(x + 2) = 0$$

$$x^2 = 0 \quad \text{or} \quad x - 3 = 0 \quad \text{or} \quad x + 2 = 0$$

$$x = 0 \qquad\qquad x = 3 \qquad\qquad x = -2$$

**Figure 8**   Print sample of Figure 7 from an Epson FX-80 printer.

## 4.4 Subscripts

A *subscripted character* (or *subscript*) is a character that is printed a half-line below the line of type it is contained in. For example, the 2 in $H_2O$ has been subscripted. To subscript a character during printing, we enclose it by ^V's.

| Command | Function |
|---------|----------|
| ^PV | Begin/end subscript |

**Comments.**   When a letter-quality printer encounters the first ^V it will move the paper up a half line and then continue printing whatever characters occur after that. When the printer encounters the second ^V it will move the paper down a half-line (returning the paper to the position before the first ^V was encountered).

Subscripts are quite common in science and mathematics. Figures 9 and 10 are, respectively, the screen display and hard copy of some text containing both subscripts and superscripts.

```
L----!----!----!----!----!----!----!----!----!----!----!--------R
^A     In  chemistry,  the  pH  of  a solution is  defined  to  be  the
negative logarithm,  to the base 10,  of the concentration of the
hydronium ion in that solution.  In symbols, it is written as:

                   pH = -log^V10^V(H^V3^VO^T+^T)

^BExample 2^B  Find the pH of a solution if (H^V3^VO^T+^T) = 2.73 x 10^T-4^T.


   ^BSolution^B              pH = -log^V10^V(H^V3^VO^T+^T)

                           = -log^V10^V(2.73 x 10^T-4^T)

                           = -[log^V10^V2.73 + log^V10^V10^T-4^T]

                           = 3.5638
```

**Figure 9** Text containing both superscripts and subscripts.

> In chemistry, the pH of a solution is defined to be the negative logarithm, to the base 10, of the concentration of the hydronium ion in that solution. In symbols, it is written as:
>
> $$pH = -\log_{10}(H_3O^+)$$
>
> **Example 2** Find the pH of a solution if $(H_3O^+) = 2.73 \times 10^{-4}$.
>
> **Solution** $\qquad pH = -\log_{10}(H_3O^+)$
>
> $$= -\log_{10}(2.73 \times 10^{-4})$$
>
> $$= -[\log_{10}2.73 + \log_{10}10^{-4}]$$
>
> $$= 3.5638$$

**Figure 10** Print sample of Figure 9 from an NEC Spinwriter with twelve-pitch thimble.

If you are using a dot-matrix printer, and you had some difficulty printing your superscripts, you will find that you have the same problems with subscripts. Your printer may print them down a whole line instead of a half line, and may ignore the $\wedge$V command if there isn't a blank line below the line that contains the characters to be subscripted.

I have installed my Epson printer so that its internal subscripted character set is accessed with the $\wedge$PE command. (As mentioned before, the $\wedge$PW command returns my Epson to its normal print mode.) Figure 11 shows the screen in Figure 9 again with the $\wedge$T's and $\wedge$V's replaced by the control characters I use to start and stop my Epson's superscript and subscript character sets. Figure 12 shows how the screen in Figure 11 looks when printed on the Epson. Remember, if you are using a dot-matrix printer, and you want to try these examples on it, you must first be sure that your printer has these alternate character sets, and then you must use the WordStar installation program to install your printer so that the alternate character sets can be accessed with the $\wedge$PQ and $\wedge$PE commands.

```
L----!----!----!----!----!----!----!----!----!----!----!--------R
     In chemistry,  the  pH of a solution is defined  to be  the
negative logarithm,  to the base 10,  of the concentration of the
hydronium ion in that solution.  In symbols, it is written as:

                  pH = -log^E10^W(H^E3^WO^Q+^W)

^BExample 2^B  Find the pH of a solution if (H^E3^WO^Q+^W) = 2.73 x 10^Q-4^W.


    ^BSolution^B          pH = -log^E10^W(H^E3^WO^Q+^W)

                         = -log^E10^W(2.73 x 10^Q-4^W)

                         = -[log^E10^W2.73 + log^E10^W10^Q-4^W]

                         = 3.5638
```

**Figure 11**  Using $\wedge$Q, $\wedge$E, and $\wedge$W to print superscripts and subscripts on an Epson FX-80 printer.

```
     In  chemistry,   the  pH  of a solution is defined  to be  the
negative logarithm,  to the base 10,  of the concentration of the
hydronium ion in that solution.  In symbols, it is written as:

                  pH = -log_{10}(H_3O^+)

Example 2  Find the pH of a solution if (H_3O^+) = 2.73 x 10^{-4}.

    Solution             pH = -log_{10}(H_3O^+)

                         = -log_{10}(2.73 x 10^{-4})

                         = -[log_{10}2.73 + log_{10}10^{-4}]

                         = 3.5638
```

**Figure 12**  Print of Figure 11 from an Epson FX-80.

## 4.5 Changing the Superscript/Subscript Roll

This section is only for those people using a letter-quality printer that can print lines on paper in increments of $\frac{1}{48}$ inch.

The control characters ^T (superscript) and ^V (subscript) are instructions to the printer to roll the paper up or down so many forty-eighths of an inch. The number of forty-eighths of an inch that the printer rolls the paper up or down is controlled by a dot command.

| Command | Function |
|---------|----------|
| .SR # | Superscript/subscript roll |

**Comments.** This dot command can be placed on any line in a file and like all dot commands the period in .SR # must appear in column 1. The line on which this command appears is not counted as a line to be printed, so any characters appearing on the same line will be ignored by the printer. The default value for # is 3, meaning a ^T or ^V will cause the printer to roll the paper down or up $\frac{3}{48}$ inch.

This dot command is useful when the text being entered contains exponents that are a mixture of numbers, letters, and plus or minus signs. Figures 13 and 14 show such an example. Notice, all the number exponents in Figure 13 are entered using special print characters for exponents, while the exponents that are letters, or plus or minus signs, are entered with the ^T command.

```
L----!----!----!----!----!----!----!----!----!----!----!--------R
.sr 2
^A^BExample 3^B  Multiply x^QE^W^Tn+^T^QQ^W and x^T-^T^QW^W^Tn^T

    ^BSolution^B   To  multiply  with the same base,  we   simply   add
    exponents

        x^QE^W^Tn+^T^QQ^Wx^T-^T^QW^W^Tn^T = x^QE^W^Tn+^T^QQ^W^T-^T^QW^W^Tn^T

                = x^Tn+^T^QR^W
```

**Figure 13**  Using a dot command with superscripts.

Example 3  Multiply $x^{3n+1}$ and $x^{-2n}$

Solution  To multiply with the same base, we simply add exponents

$$x^{3n+1}x^{-2n} = x^{3n+1-2n}$$

$$= x^{n+4}$$

**Figure 14**  Print sample of Figure 13 from an NEC Spinwriter with Tech Math/Times Roman thimble.

To see how the dot command .SR 2 enhances the hard copy in Figure 13, look at Figure 15. It is the hard copy of the screen in Figure 12 again, but this time with the .SR 2 command deleted.

**Example 3**  Multiply $x^{3n+1}$ and $x^{-2n}$

**Solution**  To multiply with the same base, we simply add exponents

$$x^{3n+1}x^{-2n} = x^{3n+1-2n}$$

$$= x^{n+4}$$

**Figure 15**  Print sample of Figure 13 (but without the dot command) from an NEC Spinwriter with Tech Math/Times Roman thimble.

As a final note, we should mention that the settings on your printer that affect the paper tension will also affect the printing of superscripts and subscripts. Sometimes, if the tension in the paper is too high, the superscript or subscript roll will be less than normal.

# 5

# Dot Commands

Dot commands are additional WordStar commands that affect the page layout and format of printed files. Although we have mentioned dot commands in previous chapters, in this chapter we list and explain all of them, so don't be surprised if it seems that we are repeating ourselves.

Among other things, dot commands can be used to control the headings, footings, margins, page numbering, and number of lines per page on your printouts. The thing that makes dot commands useful is that, with dot commands, you can easily change the format of a file that you are going to print, without having to reformat each line or paragraph of the file itself. We begin this chapter by considering the dot commands that affect the way in which the pages of a file are numbered during printing. As you will see, some of the dot commands we cover can only be used by letter-quality printers, while others can be used with any type of printer.

## 5.1 Page Numbering

During printing, WordStar will automatically number each page in the file you are printing, consecutively from the number 1. The page numbers are centered at the bottom of each page, two lines below the last possible line of text (that is, the page numbers appear six lines, or 1⅛ inches, from the bottom of an 11-inch piece of paper). The largest page number WordStar will accept is 65,533.

There are a number of situations in which you may want to turn the page numbering off. For example, it is common practice to omit the page number on the first page of a report, but number each page after that, beginning with page 2. The dot commands that follow allow you to turn the page numbering off and on.

| Command | Function |
|---------|----------|
| .OP | Omit page numbers |
| .PN # (# optional) | Number pages beginning with the number # |

**Comments.**   The letters you use to type dot commands do not have to be uppercase. As with all dot commands, the dot (the period) must be placed in column 1. WordStar will not count the line on which a dot command appears in the line count. Also, any text on the same line as a dot command will be ignored by WordStar during printing. (This allows you to place comments next to any dot command.) The .OP command instructs WordStar to stop printing the page numbers. The .PN command tells WordStar to return to page numbering. If a number between 1 and 65,533 follows the .PN command, WordStar will print the page numbers beginning with that number. For other dot commands related to page numbering, see Section 5.4 for details.

**Note.**   If you have created a file that begins with .PN 48, and you wish to begin printing on the second page of the file, you tell WordStar to begin printing on page 49, not page 2.

If you wish to change the column in which the page numbers occur, use the following command.

| Command | Function |
|---------|----------|
| .PC # | Page number in column # |

**Comments.**   This command places the page numbers in the column specified by #. If you are printing page numbers on the sixth line from the bottom of the page (the .MB and .FM commands alter the line on which the page numbers are printed), then the command .PC 10 will place each page number in column 10 of that line.

**Note.**   The column number # in the .PC # command is counted in terms of the current character width (see Section 5.2).

## 5.2 Line Height and Character Width

The following two dot commands will work with most letter-quality printers, but will be ignored by dot-matrix printers. These commands control the number of lines per page and the number of characters per line that will appear on the printed output.

| Command | Function |
|---------|----------|
| .LH # | #/48 inch per line |

**Comments.**   The default value for # is 8, which means each line will take up $\frac{8}{48}$, or $\frac{1}{6}$, inch. This gives 6 lines per inch on the printed output. This command must be placed at the beginning of a file if WordStar is to give the correct page break display. You can use it in other places in your file, but the page breaks on your printed output may not match the page breaks you see displayed on the screen. Again, this dot command will not have any affect on dot-matrix printers, but can be used with most letter-quality printers.

**Example.**   Call up any file you have created and, with the INSERT ON, type .LH 96 (RETURN) beginning in column 1 of line 1. Note how the screen changes. Move down through the file using ^C. Your screen will display page breaks every few lines. The .LH 96 command tells WordStar that the vertical distance from the beginning of one line to the beginning of the next line is $\frac{96}{48}$, or 2, inches. On 11-inch paper, we will only get four or so lines per page. (When you are done looking through this file, go back and delete the .LH 96 command.)

Although the # in .LH # can be replaced with almost any whole number, the table that follows gives some of the more common settings.

For an additional example of how this command can be used, see Chapter 6.

| Command | Line Height (in Inches) | Lines per Inch |
|---------|-------------------------|----------------|
| .LH 4   | $\frac{4}{48} = \frac{1}{12}$ | 12 |
| .LH 6   | $\frac{6}{48} = \frac{1}{8}$  | 8  |
| .LH 8   | $\frac{8}{48} = \frac{1}{6}$  | 6  |
| .LH 12  | $\frac{12}{48} = \frac{1}{4}$ | 4  |

The next dot command controls the amount of horizontal space given to each character printed by your printer. It can be used on most letter-quality printers, but not dot-matrix printers.

| Command | Function |
|---------|----------|
| .CW #   | $\frac{\#}{120}$ inches per character |

**Comments.**   The default value for # is 12, which means each character will be allotted $\frac{12}{120}$, or $\frac{1}{10}$, inch horizontally, which is equivalent to ten characters per inch. This command can be placed at the beginning of any line in a file (as long as the . is in column 1), and can be used any number of times in a file. Remember, as with all dot commands, the line in which the .CW # appears will not be printed or counted as a line of text by

WordStar. Section 6.3 has some interesting examples of how this command can be used with the alternate pitch ^A command.

**Example.** Figure 1 shows a file containing commands for line height and character width. Figure 2 shows how this file will look when printed on a letter-quality printer that is capable of interpreting these commands.

```
L----!----!----!----!----!----!----!----!----!----!----!--------R
.LH 6  THIS WILL GIVE A LINE HEIGHT OF 1/8 OF AN INCH
Using Dot Commands to
Change the Line Height

.LH 12 THIS WILL GIVE A LINE HEIGHT OF 1/4 OF AN INCH
Using Dot Commands to
Change the Line Height

.LH 4  THIS WILL GIVE A LINE HEIGHT OF 1/12 OF AN INCH
Using Dot Commands to
Change the Line Height

.LH 8  THIS IS THE DEFAULT VALUE OF 1/6 OF AN INCH

.CW 15 THIS WILL GIVE A CHARACTER WIDTH OF 1/8 OF AN INCH
Using Dot Commands to Change the Character Width

.CW 10 THIS WILL GIVE A CHARACTER WIDTH OF 1/12 OF AN INCH
Using Dot Commands to Change the Character Width

.CW 6  THIS WILL GIVE A CHARACTER WIDTH OF 1/20 OF AN INCH
Using Dot Commands to Change the Character Width

.CW 12 THIS IS THE DEFAULT VALUE OF 1/10 OF AN INCH
Using Dot Commands to Change the Character Width
```

**Figure 1** Commands for line height and character width.

```
Using Dot Commands to
Change the Line Height

Using Dot Commands to

Change the Line Height


Using Dot Commands to
Change the Line Height

Using Dot Commands to Change the Character Width

Using Dot Commands to Change the Character Width

Using Dot Commands to Change the Character Width

Using Dot Commands to Change the Character Width
```

**Figure 2** Print sample of Figure 1 from an NEC Spinwriter with twelve-pitch thimble.

## 5.3 Page Length, Top and Bottom Margins, and Page Offset

The dot commands covered in this section affect the vertical layout of the printed page. Like all dot commands, the dot must appear in column 1, and any text on the same line as the dot command will be ignored by WordStar.

| Command | Function |
|---------|----------|
| .MT # | Top margin is # lines |
| .MB # | Bottom margin is # lines |

**Comments.** The default values are .MT 3 and .MB 8, meaning that WordStar will allot three lines for the margin at the top of the page, and eight lines for the margin at the bottom of the page.

**Example.** Open a file under the file name VERTICAL.PG and enter the numbers 1 through 60 on consecutive lines beginning in column 1. (Note that the page break display appears after the number 55.)

Now move the cursor back to the beginning of the file (^QR) and make sure the INSERT is on (If off, type ^V). Type .MB 6 (RETURN) so that the dot command .MB 6 is the first line of the file. Move the cursor to the bottom of the file with the ^QC command. Note that the page break display now follows the number 57. We have added two lines to our page by changing the bottom margin from 8 to 6.

**Note.** Using the default values for the top and bottom margins and the line height, we can calculate the number of inches in our top and bottom margin as follows:

$$\text{Top margin: 3 lines} \times \frac{1 \text{ inch}}{6 \text{ lines}} = \text{½ inch}$$

$$\text{Bottom margin: 8 lines} \times \frac{1 \text{ inch}}{6 \text{ lines}} = 1\text{⅓ inches}$$

If we leave the top and bottom margins alone, but change the line height with the .LH # command, WordStar will still leave us a top margin of ½ inch and a bottom margin of 1⅓ inches. If, however, we change the number of lines in one or both of the top and bottom margins and also change the line height, we must recalculate the number of inches in the top and bottom margins. For example, if a file begins with

```
L----!----!----!----!----!----!----!----!----!----!----!--------R
.LH 6
.MT 2
.MB 4
```

then we have a file in which each line is $\frac{6}{48}$, or $\frac{1}{8}$, inch in height.

$$\text{Top margin: 2 lines} \times \frac{1 \text{ inch}}{8 \text{ lines}} = \frac{1}{4} \text{ inch}$$

$$\text{Bottom margin: 4 lines} \times \frac{1 \text{ inch}}{8 \text{ lines}} = 1\frac{1}{2} \text{ inch}$$

| Command | Function |
|---------|----------|
| .PL # | Page length is # lines |

**Comments.** The default setting is .PL 66, which means that WordStar assumes there are 66 lines per page. If each line takes up $\frac{1}{6}$ inch, then WordStar is assuming that you are using paper that is $\frac{1}{6} \times 66$, or 11 inches long. If you are using legal-size paper that is 14 inches long and printing six lines per inch, you may want to place the command .PL 84 at the beginning of your file. This will tell WordStar that each page is 84 lines long, or $84 \times \frac{1}{6} = 14$ inches in length.

As you can see, WordStar has no single command that tells how many lines of text are to be printed in the body of the text. The number of lines in the body of the text is found by subtracting the number of lines in the top and bottom margins from the number of lines in the page length. Since the default values are .PL 66, .MT 3, and .MB 8, the default value for the number of lines in the body of the text is $66 - (3 + 8) = 55$.

**Note.** As was the case with top and bottom margin commands, if the page length is left to its default value, WordStar will always give us 11 inches per page, even if we change the line height. That is, even though the .PL command is in lines (66 lines per page), if we leave it alone and change the line height to say .LH 4, which allots $\frac{4}{48}$, or $\frac{1}{12}$, inch for each line, WordStar will still give us 11 inches per page.

If you wish to change the column in which printing is to begin, use the command that follows:

| Command | Function |
|---------|----------|
| .PO # | Begin printing in column # |

**Comments.** The default for this command is .PO 8, which means that, unless you specify otherwise, WordStar will begin printing in column 8 on the paper. That is, the left margin is 8 spaces. The command .PO 16 will give a left margin of 16 spaces. If you have set the left margin in your file to 10 [^OL 10 (RETURN)] and begin the file with .PO 16, your printed pages will have a left margin of 26 spaces.

**Note.** WordStar counts the spaces in the .PO # command in terms of the character width setting in the .CW # command. If you have set the character width to ten characters per inch, then .PO 15 will give a left margin of 1.5 inches. If the character width is set to twelve characters per inch, the .PO 18 will give a left margin of 1.5 inches.

**Note.** If you use the .CW # and .PO # commands together, it makes a difference which of them comes first in the file. A file that begins with

```
L----!----!----!----!----!----!----!----!----!----!----!--------R
.CW 10
.PO 24
```

will be indented 2 inches from the left side of the paper, when printed. The first command, .CW 10, sets the character width to $^{10}/_{20}$, or $^{1}/_{2}$, inch. This gives twelve characters per inch. The .PO 24 command then instructs the printer to begin printing in column 24, which in this case is 2 inches from the left side of the paper.

On the other hand, a file that begins with

```
L----!----!----!----!----!----!----!----!----!----!----!--------R
.PO 24
.CW 10
```

will produce printed copy with twelve characters per inch, but indented 2.4 inches from the left side of the paper. The .PO 24 command is interpreted in terms of the current character width setting. Since, in this case, we changed the character width *after* we gave the .PO 24 command, the printer will begin printing in column 24 where each column width is the default $^{1}/_{10}$ inch.

## 5.4 Headings and Footings

The first two commands covered in this section are the commands that control what will be printed on the heading and footing lines of each page of a file being printed. The second two commands control the position of the heading and footing lines on the printed page.

A *heading line*, a *running head*, or just *heading*, is a line that is printed at the top of a page above the normal text. It is used to specify page numbers or information such as chapter numbers and titles. The *footing line, running foot*, or *footing* for short, is used in the same way, but appears at the bottom of each page, one or more lines below the text area.

The two commands that follow are used to place text in the heading and footing lines of each printed page.

| Command | Function |
|---|---|
| .HE (text) | Heading line is |
| .FO (text) | Footing line is |

**Comments.**    You must always include at least one space between these commands and the beginning of the message you want printed. Each command will cause the message on that line to be printed at the top or bottom of each printed page until the next .HE or .FO command is encountered. (For the exact placement of the heading and footings on the page see the .HM and .FM commands later in this section.) Print control characters for underline, boldface, and the like may be used in heading and footing lines. These commands must precede all text to be printed if they are to be printed on the first page of text. You can change them as often as you want. The default value for .HE is all blanks, and you can return to it by typing .HE with no message following. The default value for .FO is the centered page number, you can return to it by giving .FO with no message, followed by .PN.

**Note 1.**    Since the first four columns of .HE or .FO commands are used for the commands themselves (remember that at least one space must follow each of these dot commands), any message that follows will be printed four columns to the left of where it appears on the screen relative to the surrounding text.

**Note 2.**    The characters #, \, and ^K have special meanings when encountered in the heading or footing lines. The meanings are as follows:

#                        this symbol will be replaced by consecutive page numbers.

　　　\ 　　　　　　　　　this symbol will cause the next character to be
　　　　　　　　　　　　printed instead of interpreted.
　　　^K 　　　　　　　this symbol will cause all spaces preceding the
　　　　　　　　　　　　next character to be ignored if the page number is
　　　　　　　　　　　　even.

**Note 3.**　The type size used in the headings or footings corresponds to whatever character width was in effect when the heading or footing command
was given, even if the character width has been changed since.

The following examples illustrate a few of the ways in which these commands can be used.

**Example.**　This sequence of commands cause the phrase Page Number # to
be printed at the top of each page and no page number at the bottom of
each page.

```
L----!----!----!----!----!----!----!----!----!----!----!--------R
.OP
.HE Page Number #
```

The top of the fifth page of a file that begins with the two commands
above will look like this:

```
Page Number 5
```

**Example.**　For a file in which the line length is set to 65 spaces. These commands placed at the beginning of the file

```
L----!----!----!----!----!----!----!----!----!----!----!--------R
.FO Chapter 8                                    Page #
```

will cause the third page of the printed output to end like this:

```
Chapter 8                                                Page 3
```

**Example.**  The top of the fourth and fifth pages of a file that begins with

```
L----!----!----!----!----!----!----!----!----!----!----!--------R
.OF
.HE ^K                                                          #
```

will look like this:

```
4
```

```
                                                              5
```

If you glance through some textbooks you will probably find that many of them alter the message in running heads (or feet) depending on whether the page number is even or odd. For instance, it is common practice to put the chapter number and title on even-numbered pages and the section number and title on odd-numbered pages. To do this with WordStar, you have to change the headings (or footings) every time you begin a new page. One way to save yourself some time in accomplishing this is to create a separate file for each type of heading and then insert the appropriate file after each page break. (You can insert files into the file you are working on with the ^KR command, which we will cover in Section 7.5.) Since the page breaks may change if you edit the files later on, I suggest that you wait until your files are in final form before you insert these files.

Suppose you have a ten-page file that is to be Section 5 of Chapter 3, and that, because of the length of the material printed previous to this, your Section 5 is to begin with a page number of 43. If you begin your file with the dot command

```
L----!----!--- --!----!----!----!----!----!----!----!----!--------R
.PN 43
```

and then create two additional files, say HEAD3/5.EVN and HEAD3/5.ODD, where the file HEAD3/5.EVN is the single line

```
L----!----!----!----!----!----!----!----!----!----!----!--------R
.HE ^B#^B Chapter 3   Chemical Reactions
```

and the file HEAD3/5.ODD is the single line

```
L----!----!----!----!----!----!----!----!----!----!----!--------R
.HE                                    3.5  Balancing Equations ^B#^B
```

Inserting the file HEAD3/5.EVN at the beginning of each even-numbered page and the file HEAD3/5.ODD at the beginning of each odd-numbered page will cause the printed copies of pages 8 and 9 of your file to look like this:

```
50 Chapter 3   Chemical Reactions
```

```
                                       3.5   Balancing Equations 51
```

The position of the headings and footings on the printed page are controlled by two additional dot commands.

| Command | Function |
|---------|----------|
| .HM # | # blank lines between heading and beginning of text |

**Comments.**   The default setting for this command is .HM 2 which gives two blank lines between the heading line and the top line of text. If the top margin is three lines, then the default value of the .HM command would result in the heading being printed one line below the top of the paper.

| Command | Function |
|---------|----------|
| .FM # | # blank lines between last possible line of text and footing |

**Comments.**   The default setting is .FM 2, giving two blank lines between the last possible line of text and the footing. With the bottom margin set at 8 (the default for .MB #), the footing line is printed six lines from the bottom of the paper.

## 5.5 Page Breaks

The commands we cover in this section allow you to have more control over the page breaks in your file. The first command allows you to end a page and begin a new one whenever you feel it is necessary.

| Command | Function |
|---------|----------|
| .PA | Begin new page |

**Comments.**   This command can be placed anywhere in a file as long as the dot appears in column 1. This command will cause WordStar to end one page and begin another. If the page break display is ON (^OP), every .PA command will be followed by a page break display.

I use this command often. One particular place I use it is with business letters.

**Example.**   The following file is a sample of a business letter. When I print this file, I have my printer pause between pages. I print the letter first on a single sheet of paper. Then, when the printer has paused, I insert the envelope in the printer and press P on the keyboard to begin printing again. As you will see when we get to Chapter 7, instead of typing the address again, we can simply mark it as a block of text, and then use a column move to put it in the appropriate place on the screen so that it will be printed in the center of the envelope.

```
L----!----!----!----!----!----!----!----!----!----!----!--------R
.CW 10
.PO 16
.OP
```

January 1, 1984


Stephen Guty, Editor
McGraw-Hill Book Company
1221 Avenue of the Americas
New York, NY 10020

Dear Steve,

        I am writing to inform you that I have just learned how to
use the .PA command on my WordStar word processor.  I used to use
the RETURN key to get to the top of a new page.  Now that I have
discovered the .PA command, my letters have become much easier to
manage.

        Your address will follow the first page break, so I can use
my  printer to address the envelope in which I am enclosing this
letter.

                        Sincerely,



                        PAT McKEAGUE
                        Cuesta College
                        P. O. Box J
                        San Luis Obispo, CA  93403

.PA
-------------------------------------------------------------------P
Pat McKeague
Cuesta College
P. O. Box J
San Luis Obispo, CA  93403



                        Stephen Guty, Editor
                        McGraw-Hill Book Company
                        1221 Avenue of the Americas
                        New York, NY 10020
```
```

The next command lets you tell WordStar to begin a new page if there are fewer than a specified number of lines left on the current page.

| Command | Function |
|---------|----------|
| .CP # | Begin new page if less than # lines are left on the current page |

**Comments.** This command is particularly useful when entering tables or other matter that should not be split between pages. Suppose, for example, that you have created a table that is five lines in length, and that you want all five lines to appear on the same page. Placing the .CP 5 command on the line just above the first line of the table will cause a page break if fewer than five lines remain at the bottom of the current page. Therefore, even if you edit your file at a later date, the table you have created will never be split between the bottom of one page and the top of another as long as it is preceded by the .CP 5 command.

## 5.6  Miscellaneous Dot Commands

The following dot commands are usually used under special circumstances.

| Command | Function |
|---------|----------|
| .SR 3 | Subscript/superscript roll |

**Comments.** The 3 in the command .SR 3 can be replaced with any divisor of 48. When this command is encountered by your printer, all subscript or superscripts will be printed by rolling the carriage up or down the number of forty-eighths of an inch you have specified. (See Section 4.5 for an example of how this command is used.)

**Note.** Whether or not this command can be used depends on your printer. If you have a dot-matrix printer, this command will probably not work.

**Note.** In some cases the paper tension control lever on your printer also affects the position of the superscripts and subscripts. Be sure the paper tension is set correctly before you decide to alter the superscript or subscript roll.

| Command | Function |
|---------|----------|
| .UJ 1 | Microjustification on/off |

**Comments.** The default value for .UJ is 1, which means all text that is right justified is also microjustified. The command .UJ 0 will turn the micro-justification off but will not affect the right justification.

**Note.** If you have given the ∧OJ command so that the text you are typing is not being right justified, there is no need to use this command.

| Command | Function |
|---------|----------|
| .BP 1   | Bidirectional print on/off |

**Comments.** The .BP 1 command is the default command and lets your printer print bidirectionally if it can. The command .BP 0 turns off the bidirectional print so that your printer prints from left to right only.

| Command | Function |
|---------|----------|
| .. or .IG | Ignore this line |

**Comments.** This command allows you to write notes to yourself. It can be very useful if you have changed the format of your file a number of times while editing it. For another useful example of how this command can be used, see Section 2.5.

# Chapter

# 6

# Fractions

In this chapter we describe some of the different methods of entering fractions into our text files. Since there are some differences in the way in which these fractions are printed on dot-matrix printers and letter-quality printers, we give examples that show print samples from each type of printer. We begin by looking at fractions that have the same number of characters in their numerator and denominator.

## 6.1 Simple Fractions

The most efficient method of entering simple fractions is to use three screen lines for each fraction: The first line contains the numerator, the second line the fraction bar, and the third line the denominator.

### Letter-Quality Printers

If we are using a letter-quality printer that is capable of interpreting the dot command for line height, then we squeeze the lines together during printing by instructing the printer to print twelve lines per inch, instead of the usual six lines per inch. Setting the line height to 4 (.LH 4) will cause the printer to print twelve lines per inch.

The advantage of this method of entering fractions is that what you see on the screen is almost exactly what you will see on the printed page. I usually set line spacing to 2 (^OS 2), so I will be sure to leave a blank line between any text I type. Remember, if you change the line height in the middle of a file, the page breaks you see on your screen may not be correct. Because of this, I set the line height at the beginning of the file and then leave it that way. Figure 1 shows the screen display of a file containing some simple fractions.

```
L----!----!----!----!----!----!----!----!----!----!----!--------R
.LH 4   PRINTER WILL PRINT 12 LINES PER INCH
.CW 10  PRINTER WILL PRINT 12 CHARACTERS PER INCH

                3   x - 1
Example 1  Add  - + -----.
                4   x + 2


     Solution:   We add fractions by finding the LCD, changing to

     equivalent fractions, and adding numerators.


          3   x - 1   3 x + 2   x - 1 4
          - + ----- = -^T.^T----- + -----^T.^T-
          4   x + 2   4 x + 2   x + 2 4


                     3x + 6   4x - 4
                   = ------ + ------
                     4x + 8   4x + 8


                     7x + 1
                   = ------
                     4x + 8
```

**Figure 1**  Simple fractions.

Note that we have superscripted two periods so they print as multiplication dots. Whenever control characters appear on a line that also contains part of a fraction, it is a good idea to use the $^\wedge$OD command to hide the control characters; that way you can be sure you have the numerators and denominators aligned.

Figure 2 shows how the screen in Figure 1 will look when printed on an NEC Spinwriter with the Tech Math/Times Roman thimble.

Example 1   Add $\frac{3}{4} + \frac{x-1}{x+2}$.

Solution:   We add fractions by finding the LCD, changing to equivalent fractions, and combining numerators.

$$\frac{3}{4} + \frac{x-1}{x+2} = \frac{3}{4} \cdot \frac{x+2}{x+2} + \frac{x-1}{x+2} \cdot \frac{4}{4}$$

$$= \frac{3x+6}{4x+8} + \frac{4x-4}{4x+8}$$

$$= \frac{7x+1}{4x+8}$$

**Figure 2**  Print sample of Figure 1 from an NEC Spinwriter with Tech Math/Times Roman thimble.

I usually go over the fraction bars with a ruler and a fine-point pen. If you want the fraction bars filled in completely by your printer, you can use superscripted underline symbols instead of hyphens. If you use the underline symbols, be sure to give the ^OD command after you have finished entering your text, to hide all the ^T's. You want to be sure your numerators and denominators are aligned. Figures 3 and 4 show the screen display and print sample respectively, when the hyphens are replaced by superscripted underline symbols.

```
L----!----!----!----!----!----!----!----!----!----!--------R
.LH 4
.CW 10
                3   x - 1
Example 1   Add ^T_^T + ^T_____^T.
                4   x + 2

    Solution:   We add fractions by finding the LCD, changing to

    equivalent fractions, and adding numerators.


            3   x - 1   3   x + 2   x - 1   4
            ^T_^T + ^T_____^T = ^T_ . _____^T + ^T_____ . _^T
            4   x + 2   4   x + 2   x + 2   4


                3x + 6   4x - 4
              = ^T_____^T + ^T_____^T
                4x + 8   4x + 8


                7x + 1
              = ^T_____^T
                4x + 8
```

**Figure 3**  Filled-in fraction bars.

Example 1   Add $\frac{3}{4} + \frac{x-1}{x+2}$.

Solution:  We add fractions by finding the LCD, changing to equivalent fractions, and adding numerators.

Solution:  $\frac{3}{4} + \frac{x-1}{x+2} = \frac{3}{4} \cdot \frac{x+2}{x+2} + \frac{x-1}{x+2} \cdot \frac{4}{4}$

$= \frac{3x+6}{4x+8} + \frac{4x-4}{4x+8}$

$= \frac{7x+1}{4x+8}$

**Figure 4**  Print sample of Figure 3 from an NEC Spinwriter with Tech Math/Times Roman thimble.

**Note.** The width of the hyphen symbol will vary among print wheels. If you are using a print wheel with a wide hyphen, your hard copy will probably look better if you use the superscripted underline symbols for your fraction bars.

There are other methods of typing simple fractions. For example, the fraction ¾ can be printed vertically by superscripting an underlined 3 (^PT^PS3^PS^PT) and then overstriking a subscripted 4 (^PH^PV4 ^PV). It will print like this:

$$\frac{3}{4}$$

I don't use this method because I don't think the hard copy looks as nice, and the number of control characters take too long to type and are confusing to look at on the screen. Even if you hide the control characters using the ^OD command, the 4 you are overstriking will still appear on the screen. WordStar will remember that it is not taking up an additional space, but it is still difficult to align other fractions and expressions around it.

### Dot-Matrix Printers

Since dot-matrix printers cannot take advantage of the dot command that controls the line height, it is not as easy to squeeze the numerator and denominator of the fractions in Figure 1 together. If you are using a dot-matrix printer that is installed so that it prints superscripts and subscripts by rolling the paper up and down a half line, then you can get around this problem by subscripting the top lines of the fractions, and superscripting the bottom lines. Figure 5 shows the text that was shown in Figure 1, but this time it is adjusted for printing on a dot-matrix printer. Again, if you are going to use this method of formatting fractions, be sure to give the ^OD command to hide the control characters after you have finished typing in the text, so that you can check to see that the numerators and denominators are aligned.

Figure 6 shows how the screen in Figure 5 will look when printed on an Epson FX-80 printer. Note that the Epson must be installed so that it prints superscripts and subscripts by rolling the paper up and down a half line. If your dot-matrix printer is installed so that it prints superscripts and subscripts on separate lines, your printout will not look like this.

```
L----!----!----!----!----!----!----!----!----!----!----!--------R
                ^V3    x - 1^V
    Example 1   Add - + -----.
                ^T4    x + 2^T
```

    Solution:   We add fractions by finding the LCD, changing to
    equivalent fractions, and adding numerators.

```
            ^V3    x - 1   3 x + 2   x - 1 4^V
            - + ----- = -^T.^T----- + -----^T.^T-
            ^T4    x + 2   4 x + 2   x + 2 4^T

                    ^V3x + 6   4x - 4^V
                  = ------ + ------
                    ^T4x + 8   4x + 8^T

                    ^V7x + 1^V
                  = ------
                    ^T4x + 8^T
```

**Figure 5**   Screen display of Figure 1 adjusted for use with a dot-matrix printer.

**Figure 6**   Print sample of Figure 5 from an Epson FX-80 printer.

## 6.2 Fractions with Exponents

Figure 7 shows the screen display for some fractions that contain exponents. Notice that the line height is set at 6 instead of 4. Setting the line
height to 6 will give a little more room between lines so that the exponents
in the denominator do not overlap the fraction bar. The screen display in
Figure 7 is what you would use if you were going to print the file on a
letter-quality printer that interprets the line height command. Figure 8 is
the corresponding print sample from an NEC Spinwriter.

```
L----!----!----!----!----!----!----!----!----!----!----!--------R
.LH 6    PRINTER WILL PRINT 8 LINES PER INCH
.CW 10   PRINTER WILL PRINT 12 CHARACTERS PER INCH


                                     x^T2^T - 4
Example 2  Reduce to lowest terms    ------.
                                     x^T3^T - 8


    Solution   We   begin  by factoring both  the  numerator  and

    denominator.   Then  we divide out any factors they have   in

    common.



       x^T2^T - 4     (x - 2)(x + 2)         Factor the numerator
       ------ = ---------------------
       x^T3^T - 8  (x - 2)(x^T2^T + 2x + 4)    and denominator



              x + 2                    Divide out the
        = -----------
          x^T2^T + 2x + 4              common factor (x - 2)
```

**Figure 7** Screen display of fractions with exponents to be used with a letter-quality printer.

Example 2  Reduce to lowest terms $\dfrac{x^2 - 4}{x^3 - 8}$.

Solution  We begin by factoring both the numerator and denominator.  Then we divide out any factors they have in common.

$$\frac{x^2 - 4}{x^3 - 8} = \frac{(x - 2)(x + 2)}{(x - 2)(x^2 + 2x + 4)}$$ Factor the numerator and denominator

$$= \frac{x + 2}{x^2 + 2x + 4}$$ Divide out the common factor $(x - 2)$

**Figure 8** Print sample of Figure 7 from an NEC Spinwriter with Tech Math/Times Roman thimble.

Figures 9 and 10 show the screen display and corresponding print sample of the same text shown in the previous two figures, but this time with the exponents entered using the special characters available on the NEC Spinwriter Tech Math/Times Roman thimble. Note that the line height in Figure 9 has been set back to 4.

```
L----!----!----!----!----!----!----!----!----!----!--------R
.LH 4    PRINTER WILL PRINT 12 LINES PER INCH
.CW 10   PRINTER WILL PRINT 12 CHARACTERS PER INCH


                              x^QW^W - 4
Example 2  Reduce to lowest terms  ------.
                              x^QE^W - 8


   Solution   We  begin  by factoring both   the   numerator   and

   denominator.   Then  we divide out any factors they have   in

   common.



      x^QW^W - 4      (x - 2)(x + 2)         Factor the numerator
      ------ = --------------------
      x^QE^W - 8   (x - 2)(x^QW^W + 2x + 4)     and denominator



           x + 2                    Divide out the
      = -----------
        x^QW^W + 2x + 4             common factor (x - 2)
```

**Figure 9** Text containing both superscripts and subscripts.

Example 2  Reduce to lowest terms $\dfrac{x^2 - 4}{x^3 - 8}$.

Solution  We begin by factoring both the numerator and denominator. Then we divide out any factors they have in common.

$$\frac{x^2 - 4}{x^3 - 8} = \frac{(x - 2)(x + 2)}{(x - 2)(x^2 + 2x + 4)}$$ Factor the numerator and denominator

$$= \frac{x + 2}{x^2 + 2x + 4}$$ Divide out the common factor $(x - 2)$

**Figure 10** Print sample of Figure 9 from an NEC Spinwriter with Tech Math/Times Roman thimble.

## Dot-Matrix Printers

Since the line height dot command will not work with dot-matrix printers, we have to do a little extra work to get a nice printout of fractions that contain exponents. I owe the idea in the next example to Lee Welch, who reviewed the manuscript for this book. Lee spent quite a bit of time trying to get his C. Itoh Prowriter printer to print exponents and fractions with the numerators and denominators as close to the fraction bar as possible.

Figure 11 is the screen display of the text in Figures 7 and 9, but this time with everything in the numerators subscripted except the exponents. Instead of raising the exponents in the numerator a half line, we lower everything around them. In a way, it is the opposite of what you usually do to get exponents. Figure 12 is the print sample of the screen in Figure 11 as it would look if printed on an Epson FX-80 printer.

```
L----!----!----!----!----!----!----!----!----!----!----!--------R

                                      ^Vx^V2^V - 4^V
Example 2  Reduce to lowest terms   ------.
                                      x^T3^T - 8

   Solution   We   begin  by factoring both  the  numerator  and
   denominator.   Then  we divide out any factors they have  in
   common.

        ^Vx^V2^V - 4      (x - 2)(x + 2)        Factor the numerator^V
        ------ = --------------------
        x^V3^T - 8   (x - 2)(x^T2^T + 2x + 4)    and denominator

                  ^Vx + 2                   Divide out the^V
             = -----------
               x^T2^T + 2x + 4              common factor (x - 2)
```

**Figure 11**  Screen display of fractions with exponents achieved by subscripting everything in numerators except the exponents.

```
                                            x^2 - 4
Example 2   Reduce to lowest terms        --------.
                                            x^3 - 8

   Solution    We   begin  by factoring both   the  numerator   and
   denominator.    Then  we divide out any factors they have   in
   common.

      x^2 - 4      (x - 2)(x + 2)           Factor the numerator
      ------- = ----------------------
      x^3 - 8    (x - 2)(x^2 + 2x + 4)      and denominator

               x + 2                        Divide out the
         = -------------
           x^2 + 2x + 4                     common factor (x - 2)
```

**Figure 12**  Print sample of Figure 11 from an Epson FX-80 printer.

## 6.3 Fractions with Exponents and Subscripts

Fractions that contain both exponents and subscripts are actually easier to format than fractions that contain only exponents. Figure 13 shows the screen display for an example from chemistry. The exponents are printed using the ^T command, and the subscripts are printed using the ^V. Figure 14 shows the corresponding print sample for a letter-quality printer. The formatting of the fractions in this example would be no different if we were using a dot-matrix printer.

```
L----!----!----!----!----!----!----!----!----!----!----!--------R
.CW 10
Example 3   How many molecules of H^V2^VO are in 26.0 grams of water?

    Solution:   We convert from grams H^V2^VO to moles H^V2^VO, to mole-
    cules H^V2^VO, using the conversion factors below.


        1 mole H^V2^VO      and     6.02 x 10^T23^T   molecules H^V2^VO
        -----------                 --------------------------
        18.0 g H^V2^VO                  1 mole H^V2^VO


                    1 mole H^V2^VO   6.03 x 10^T23^T   molecules H^V2^VO
    26.0 g H^V2^VO x ---------- x --------------------------
                     18.0 g H^V2^VO           1 mole H^V2^VO
```

**Figure 13**  A chemistry example.

$$\text{Example 3} \quad \text{How many molecules of } H_2O \text{ are in 26.0 grams of water?}$$

Solution:   We convert from grams $H_2O$ to moles $H_2O$, to molecules $H_2O$, using the conversion factors below.

$$\frac{1 \text{ mole } H_2O}{18.0 \text{ g } H_2O} \quad \text{and} \quad \frac{6.02 \times 10^{23} \text{ molecules } H_2O}{1 \text{ mole } H_2O}$$

$$26.0 \text{ g } H_2O \text{ x } \frac{1 \text{ mole } H_2O}{18.0 \text{ g } H_2O} \text{ x } \frac{6.03 \times 10^{23} \text{ molecules } H_2O}{1 \text{ mole } H_2O}$$

**Figure 14**  Print sample of Figure 13 from an NEC Spinwriter with Tech Math/Times Roman thimble.

As a final note for this section, let's look at **Example 3** again, but this time using the special print thimble (the Tech Math/Times Roman thimble on my NEC Spinwriter printer) to print the exponents and subscripts. In order to print the subscript 2 in $H_2O$ using this thimble, we enclose the ^QW^W with ^V's. That way, what would normally print as a small exponent 2 is now a small subscript 2. Figure 15 shows the screen display and Figure 16 shows the print sample that corresponds to it. Note that we have also changed the line height to twelve lines per inch.

```
L----!----!----!----!----!----!----!----!----!----!----!--------R
.LH 4
.CW 10
Example 2   How many molecules of H^V^QW^W^VO are in 26.0 grams of water?


    Solution:   We convert from grams H^V^QW^W^VO to moles H^V^QW^W^VO, to mole-

    cules H^V^QW^W^VO, using the conversion factors below.


       1 mole H^V^QW^W^VO      and    6.02 x 10^QWE^W   molecules H^V^QW^W^VO
       -----------                    ---------------------------
       18.0 g H^V^QW^W^VO                    1 mole H^V^QW^W^VO


                   1 mole H^V^QW^W^VO   6.03 x 10^QWE^W   molecules H^V^QW^W^VO
       26.0 g H^V^QW^W^VO x ----------- x ---------------------------
                   18.0 g H^V^QW^W^VO             1 mole H^V^QW^W^VO
```

**Figure 15**   Screen display of chemistry example prepared for the NEC Spinwriter.

Example 3   How many molecules of $H_2O$ are in 26.0 grams of water?

Solution:   We convert from grams $H_2O$ to moles $H_2O$, to molecules $H_2O$, using the conversion factors below.

$$\frac{1 \text{ mole } H_2O}{18.0 \text{ g } H_2O} \quad \text{and} \quad \frac{6.02 \times 10^{23} \text{ molecules } H_2O}{1 \text{ mole } H_2O}$$

$$26.0 \text{ g } H_2O \times \frac{1 \text{ mole } H_2O}{18.0 \text{ g } H_2O} \times \frac{6.03 \times 10^{23} \text{ molecules } H_2O}{1 \text{ mole } H_2O}$$

**Figure 16**   Print sample of Figure 15 from an NEC Spinwriter with Tech Math/Times Roman thimble.

## 6.4  Aligning Numerator and Denominator

The example that we give in this section is intended for use with letter-quality printers that can interpret the dot command for character width. What we have to say here does not apply to dot-matrix printers.

Many simple fractions like $^3\!/_5$ can be a problem if you want them printed vertically with the numerator and denominator centered over one another. The problem is that one term has an even number of characters, while the other has an odd number of characters, and WordStar has no direct provision for half-spacing. You can get around this, however, by changing the character width so that you can enter a space or two that is half the width of a normal space. To do so, we use a dot command in combination with the commands that follow.

| Command | Function |
|---------|----------|
| ^PA | Select alternate pitch |
| ^PN | Select normal pitch |

**Comments.**   These are print commands. They will appear on the screen as ^A and ^N. To select an alternate pitch, you give the ^PA command and then follow it with a .CW $x$ command. For example, if we want an alternate pitch of twenty-four characters per inch, we give the following sequence of commands:

```
L----!----!----!----!----!----!----!----!----!----!----!--------R
^A
.CW 5    THIS GIVES US 24 CHARACTERS PER INCH
```

To return to our normal pitch we simply type ^PN. But now, every time we type ^PA the printer will automatically begin printing twenty-four characters per inch, no matter where we are on the page.

Suppose we want to set up our text so that it normally prints twelve characters per inch, and the alternate pitch is twenty-four characters per inch. The following sequence of commands, placed at the beginning of a file, will do just that:

```
L----!----!----!----!----!----!----!----!----!----!----!--------R
.CW 10   THIS GIVES 12 CHARACTERS PER INCH FOR THE NORMAL PITCH
^A       CHANGE TO ALTERNATE PITCH
.CW 5    THIS SETS THE ALTERNATE PITCH TO 24 CHARCTERS PER INCH
^N       RETURN TO NORMAL PITCH
```

Now we can type the fraction $^3\!/_5$ vertically with the 5 aligned between the 3 and the $x$. To do so, we type the numerator, fraction bar, and denominator on separate lines with the 5 below the $x$. We precede the space before the 5 with the ^A command to change the character width to twenty characters per inch. We return to the normal ten characters per inch with the ^N command. (Remember, to insert the ^A command in your text, type ^PA.)

| **Screen** | **Print** |
|---|---|
| 3× | 3 × |
| -- | -- |
| ^A n5^N | 5 |

Figures 17 and 18 show an example from trigonometry that contains fractions in which some adjustment of the character width must be made in order to align the numerators and denominators. Notice also that we obtained the plus or minus sign (±) by simply underlining a + sign.

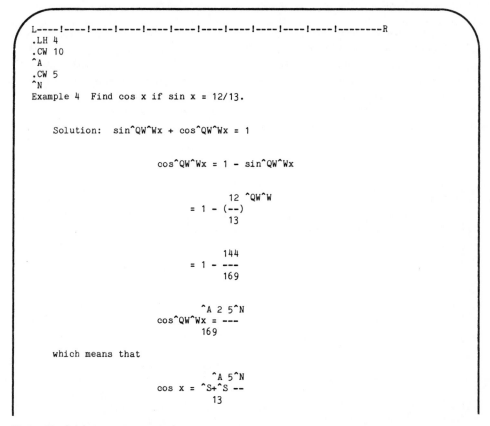

```
L----!----!----!----!----!----!----!----!----!----!--------R
.LH 4
.CW 10
^A
.CW 5
^N
Example 4  Find cos x if sin x = 12/13.


    Solution:  sin^QW^Wx + cos^QW^Wx = 1


               cos^QW^Wx = 1 - sin^QW^Wx


                      12 ^QW^W
               = 1 - (--)
                      13


                      144
               = 1 - ---
                      169


                      ^A 2 5^N
          cos^QW^Wx = ---
                      169

  which means that

                      ^A 5^N
          cos x = ^S+^S --
                      13
```

**Figure 17**  A trigonometry example.

$$\text{Example 4} \quad \text{Find } \cos x \text{ if } \sin x = 12/13.$$

$$\text{Solution:} \quad \sin^2 x + \cos^2 x = 1$$

$$\cos^2 x = 1 - \sin^2 x$$

$$= 1 - \left(\frac{12}{13}\right)^2$$

$$= 1 - \frac{144}{169}$$

$$\cos^2 x = \frac{25}{169}$$

$$\text{which means that}$$

$$\cos x = \pm \frac{5}{13}$$

**Figure 18**  Print sample of Figure 17 from an NEC Spinwriter with Tech Math/Times Roman thimble.

## 6.5  Using Special Print Thimbles to Produce Fractions

For our final example in this chapter we give an alternative to using the regular keyboard numbers for fractions. Instead of the regular keyboard numbers, we use the small exponents found on the Technical Math/Times Roman thimble for the NEC Spinwriter printer. Figure 19 shows how this is done. Notice that the line height is set at 4, the subscript/superscript roll is set at 2, and the lines containing numerators are subscripted. These

```
L----!----!----!----!----!----!----!----!----!----!--------R
.LH 4
.SR 2
.CW 10

                     ^V    ^QQ^W       ^QQ^W      ^QQ^W       ^QQ^W ^V
Example 5  Simplify (1 - -)(1 - -)(1 - -)(1 - -).
                     ^QW^W       ^QE^W      ^QR^W       ^QT^W


    Solution:   Subtracting  inside each set of parentheses  and

then dividing out common factors we have


     ^V   ^QQ^W      ^QQ^W      ^QQ^W      ^QQ^W     ^QQ^W ^QW^W ^QE^W ^QR^W ^V
    (1 - -)(1 - -)(1 - -)(1 - -) = (-)(-)(-)(-)
         ^QW^W       ^QE^W      ^QR^W       ^QT^W     ^QW^W ^QE^W ^QR^W ^QT^W


                        ^V  ^QQ^W ^V
                      = -
                        ^QT^W
```

**Figure 19**  Screen display of alternative way of keyboarding fractions.

settings place the numerators and denominators of the fractions at equal distances from the fraction bars. Figure 19 shows the screen display with the control characters showing, while Figure 20 shows the same screen with the control characters hidden. Figure 21 is the corresponding print sample.

```
L----!----!----!----!----!----!----!----!----!----!----!--------R
.LH 2
.SR 2
.CW 10

                    V   Q       Q       Q      Q V
Example 5  Simplify (1 - -)(1 - -)(1 - -)(1 - -).
                    W       E       R       T


    Solution:   Subtracting  inside each set of parentheses  and

then dividing out common factors we have

        V   Q       Q       Q       Q      Q W  E  R V
        (1 - -)(1 - -)(1 - -)(1 - -) = (-)(-)(-)(-)
        W       E       R       T      W  E  R  T


                            V Q V
                          = -
                            T
```

**Figure 20**   Screen display of Figure 19 with control characters hidden.

Example 5   Simplify $(1 - \frac{1}{2})(1 - \frac{1}{3})(1 - \frac{1}{4})(1 - \frac{1}{5})$.

Solution: Subtracting inside each set of parentheses and then dividing out common factors we have

$$(1 - \tfrac{1}{2})(1 - \tfrac{1}{3})(1 - \tfrac{1}{4})(1 - \tfrac{1}{5}) = (\tfrac{1}{2})(\tfrac{2}{3})(\tfrac{3}{4})(\tfrac{4}{5})$$

$$= \tfrac{1}{5}$$

**Figure 21**   Print sample of Figures 19 and 20 from an NEC Spinwriter with Tech Math/ Times Roman thimble.

# 7

# Finding and Moving Text

In this chapter we cover a number of commands that are very useful for moving quickly to specific places in a file you have already created, and for manipulating blocks of text within a file. We will also see how it is possible to find text anywhere in a file and then change, delete, or move it with just a few simple commands. Some of the commands covered in this chapter were previously covered in Chapter 1, but here they are explained in more detail.

## 7.1 Finding Characters and Strings

With WordStar, you have the ability to search a file for a specific character or string of characters, no matter where you are in that file. To ask WordStar to search the file you are working on, give the following command:

| Command | Function |
|---------|----------|
| ^QF | Find a string of characters |

**Comments.** When you give this command, WordStar will respond with the following message:

FIND?

You respond with the characters or string of characters you want WordStar to find in the file you are editing. For example, if you wanted WordStar to find the phrase "Problem Set 3.2,"you would simply type

*Problem Set 3.2,* followed by RETURN, and WordStar would then respond with

```
OPTIONS (? FOR INFO)
```

The most common response to this question is to simply press the RETURN key. WordStar would then search the file you are working on, from the current cursor position, until it finds the phrase "Problem Set 3.2."

**Note.** You can bypass the Options question completely by simply pressing the ESCAPE key after you have given WordStar the character string you want it to find. That is, instead of typing in your character string and pressing RETURN, you type in your character string and press ESCAPE.

After WordStar has found the first occurrence of the string in question, you can ask it to find the next occurrence with the following command.

| Command | Function |
|---------|----------|
| ^L | Find again |

**Comments.** You can give the command ^L at any time after you have given WordStar a character string to find. WordStar will then continue to search the file until it finds the next occurrence of that string.

If the phrase "Problem Set 3.2" does not occur from your present cursor position to the end of the file, WordStar will indicate so with the following message:

```
*** NOT FOUND: "Problem Set 3.2" *** Press ESCAPE Key
```

**Options.** Now let's digress for a moment. After you have given WordStar a character string to find and pressed RETURN, you will be asked if there are any other options you would like to be in effect. If you type a question mark in response to the Options question, following it with RETURN, WordStar will list the available options like this:

```
    Normally press RETURN only, or enter one or more of:
number=repeat count, B=search Backwards, W=whole Words only,
U=ignore case, N=replace w/o asking, G=replace in entire file.
```

You can specify as many of these options as you would like. After you specify one or more of these options, press RETURN. The following paragraphs provide an explanation of each of these options.

To use the first option, *number = repeat count,* you simply specify a number. WordStar will then find that occurrence of the phrase you are looking for. For example, if "Problem Set 3.2" occurred twenty times in the file you were searching, and you only wanted WordStar to find the sixth occurrence of it, you would respond to the Options question by typing the number 6 followed by RETURN. WordStar would then find the sixth occurrence of the phrase "Problem Set 3.2" past your current cursor position. Note that this option has a different effect with the Find and replace command that we cover in the next section.

Responding to the Options question with B (RETURN) will cause WordStar to search your file from the current cursor position to the beginning of the file. That is, WordStar will search your file backward from the current cursor position.

The *whole words only* option is particularly useful. If you wanted to search a file for the word *sent,* giving the option W (RETURN) would cause WordStar to find *sent* only when it appeared with a space before or after it; that is, it would not find the words *present* or *absent.*

If you type U (RETURN), WordStar will find not only "Problem Set 3.2," but "problem set 3.2," "PROBLEM SET 3.2," and any other phrase containing those characters without regard to uppercase or lowercase. This option is useful if you want to find a phrase that may or may not begin a sentence in your file.

The last two options, N and G, are used mainly with the Find and replace command, which we cover in the next section.

## 7.2  Find and Replace

The WordStar command that follows gives you the ability to find a phrase or a character string and then replace it with another phrase or string. As with the Find command, there are a number of options available with this command.

| Command | Function |
|---------|----------|
| ^QA | Find and replace |

**Comments.**   When you give this command, WordStar will respond by asking you for the character string you want to replace. It does so with the question

FIND?

You then type in the character string you want replaced followed by RETURN. WordStar will then ask you for the new character string with the question

REPLACE WITH?

You respond by typing in the new character string, followed by RETURN. WordStar will then ask you for any options you would like. If you press RETURN in response to the options question, WordStar will find the first occurrence of your original string and then ask you if you want to replace it with your new string. If you type Y, WordStar will replace the original character string with the new string. If you type N, WordStar will not replace it. Typing ^L will get you to the next occurrence of your original string, and you will be asked again if you want it replaced or not.

The options covered in Section 7.1 for the Find command can also be used with the Find and replace command. However, the *number = repeat count* option, if used with the Find and replace command, will cause WordStar to find and replace the first *n* occurrences of the strings you have specified, instead of just the *n*th occurrence.

In addition to the options covered under the Find command in the previous section, there are two other options available with Find and replace. The first is the N option, which replaces your original string of characters with the new string without asking for a yes or no response. The second is the G option, which searches the whole file from the beginning to the end regardless of where the cursor currently is.

**Example.**    I use the Find and replace command quite often. For example, if I am typing a section in which the exponent 2 occurs frequently, instead of typing ^T2^T each time I want an exponent 2, I type an asterisk (*). When I am done with the whole section, I have WordStar find every occurrence of * and replace it with ^T2^T. I usually do this with the G and N options in effect. Not only does this save me typing time, but I know that each of my exponents will be typed correctly.

**Note.**    If you have a large number of occurrences of a character string you want replaced, you can use the G and N options to have WordStar do the replacement each time without asking for further instructions. When you use these options, you will notice that WordStar shows you each replacement even though it doesn't ask you if you want it done. You can speed up the process considerably by giving another command after WordStar has begun the replacement process. I usually give the ^S command, but any command that does not put a character on the screen will do. Giving another command while WordStar is finding and replacing a character string causes WordStar to stop updating the screen with each of the changes it makes. You will be surprised at how quickly WordStar makes the replacements you specify, when it no longer has to show you each replacement.

### Special Characters That Can Be Embedded in the Find String

There are a number of special characters you can embed in your find string when using the Find or the Find and replace commands. These are control characters that allow you to find general characters rather than specific characters.

| Command in find string | Function |
|---|---|
| ^P^A | Find any character at position of ^A |

**Comments.**    To give this command in a find string, you must hold down the CONTROL key while you type both the P and the A. When you type ^P^A, you will see ^A on the screen at the cursor postions. This tells WordStar that the string you want to find can have any character at that particular position.

**Example.**    If you want WordStar to find any string in which the first two letters are *se,* then your find string would look like se^A. WordStar would then find *see, sea, set,* and any other string that began with *se.*

**Note.**    WordStar cannot find the character ^A as used in a file to change to alternate pitch. Any ^A in a find string must occur as described above.

| Command in find string | Function |
|---|---|
| ^P^S | Find any symbol, other than a letter or a number at position of ^S |

**Comments.**    Again, you must hold down the CONTROL key while you type both the P and the S. Typing ^P^S in a find string will cause ^S to occur at the cursor position. WordStar will then find the string you have specified, with any character except a letter or number where the ^S appears in the string.

**Example.**    If you have a file that contains expressions like s=t, s<t, or x>t, and you want WordStar to find each of them, type s^St in response to the Find question. WordStar will then find the above phrases, but will ignore the phrases set, sit, or any other phrase that has a letter or number between the s and t.

**Note.** WordStar cannot find the character ∧S as used in a file to begin or end underlining. Any ∧S in a find string will be interpreted as described above.

| Command in find string | Function |
|---|---|
| ∧Ox | Find any character other than x |

**Comments.** Typing ∧O, not ∧P∧O, while giving WordStar a string of characters to find will cause ∧O to appear at the cursor position. When WordStar is finding the string you have typed, it will find all strings except those that have the character that follows the ∧O at that position in the string.

| Command in find string | Function |
|---|---|
| ∧N | Find carriage return and line feed |

**Comments.** Insert ∧N in a string by typing ∧N, not ∧P∧N. This causes WordStar to find carriage returns accompanied by line feeds, which is what is put into your files when you press the RETURN key on your keyboard. This command is useful if you want to find the end of a paragraph, or where you have double-spaced (two ∧N's in a row) in a normally single-spaced file, or when you want to convert a WordStar file to a file that can be read by another word processing program that does not use the same symbols for carriage returns and line feeds.

## 7.3 Working with Blocks of Text

We showed how to mark a block of text in Chapter 1. To review, here are the commands to do so.

| Command | Function |
|---|---|
| ∧KB | Mark beginning of block |
| ∧KK | Mark end of block |

**Comments.** On the IBM Personal Computer, pressing function key F7 is equivalent to the giving the first command, ∧KB, while function key F8 is equivalent to the second command, ∧KK. When you give the command

∧KB, WordStar will insert ⟨B⟩ at the cursor position. What happens when you give the command ∧KK depends on the kind of terminal you have. If your terminal is capable of *highlighting* (some text is lighter than other text) or *reverse video* (black characters on a light background), you will see the block you have just marked displayed that way. If your terminal is not capable of highlighting or reverse video, then you will see ⟨K⟩ displayed at the end of each line of the block and a ⟨B⟩ displayed at the beginning of each line in your block. (Note that some versions of WordStar will display only the first ⟨B⟩ and the last ⟨K⟩ of the marked block.)

Once you have marked the block of text you want to work with, you can move it, copy it, or delete it, among other things. The following paragraphs explain the commands that affect the marked block of text.

| Command | Function |
|---------|----------|
| ∧KV | Move marked block to cursor position |

**Comments.**   You can move a marked block of text to a new position in a file by giving the command ∧KV. After you have marked a block of text, move the cursor to the place in the file where you want to move the marked block. Next type ∧KV. WordStar will then remove the marked block from its current position and rewrite it at the cursor position. The marked block is inserted at the cursor position, regardless of whether the INSERT is on or off.

| Command | Function |
|---------|----------|
| ∧KC | Copy marked block to cursor position |

**Comments.**   In some cases, you may want to keep the marked block in its current position and also copy it to another position. The ∧KC command will accomplish this. Copying a marked block allows you to place repeated phrases, paragraphs, or tables in numerous places in your file without having to retype them each time.

**Note.**   If you are working in a large file and want to move a marked block of text a large distance, you may find that it takes WordStar longer than you like. Also, if you have small capacity diskettes, you may get a "disk full" error, which can cause real problems. You can avoid these difficulties, by using the commands covered in Section 7.4.

Once you have moved or copied your block of text, you will notice that it is still displayed as a marked block. That is, it will still have the block markers ⟨B⟩ and ⟨K⟩, or be in reverse video or half-intensity. You can hide the block markers and return the marked block back to normal viewing with the following commands.

| Command | Function |
|---------|----------|
| ^KH | Hide block markers |

**Comments.** If your marked block is displayed in half-intensity or reverse video, or with ⟨B⟩ and ⟨K⟩, giving this command will return the block to normal viewing. Note, however, that you cannot do anything with the block unless it is marked on the screen. Giving the command a second time, after you have hidden the markers, will restore the markers.

| Command | Function |
|---------|----------|
| ^KY | Delete marked block |

**Comments.** Use this command to delete a block of text. I use this quite often when I am writing letters. If I have previously sent a letter to someone and need to write to the same person again, I usually call up the previous letter, mark everything from the salutation to the closing, and then delete that block. That way I don't have to retype the dot commands at the beginning of the letter or the headings that contain the person's title and address.

There is one last option you can use with your block commands. This option is available only if you have version 3.0 or higher of WordStar. It is the *column move* option and is accessed with the following command.

| Command | Function |
|---------|----------|
| ^KN | Column mode on/off |

**Comments.** This is a toggle command. Normally, the column mode is in the OFF state. To turn it on, type ^KN. To then turn it off again, type ^KN again. If you want to move, copy, or delete a block of text in the column mode, you must turn the column mode on before you mark the block you want to work with. Once the column mode is on, you can mark a column or columns of text by first placing the cursor at the beginning of the column you want to mark and then typing ^KB as usual. To mark the end of the column block, you move the cursor one character past the last character in the last column you want to mark. WordStar will then mark everything in the rectangle whose upper left hand corner is ⟨B⟩ and whose lower right hand corner is ⟨K⟩. Now you can move, copy, or delete the column block you have marked. When the column mode is on, the maximum width of a column you can mark is 240 characters. Also, there is a limit to the total number of characters in the block. That limit depends not only on the number of characters in the column block but also on the number of characters surrounding the block. If the block you mark is too large, WordStar will let you know by displaying:

BLOCK TOO LONG

If this happens, simply move, copy, or delete the material in your block in smaller quantities, by marking smaller blocks, and then moving them one at a time.

**Example.**  Figure 1 shows a screen display with the positions at which the cursor should be placed in order to mark the beginning and end of the column block to be moved. In addition, Figure 1 shows the position to which the marked block is to be moved. Figure 2 shows the screen display that results when the ∧KV command is then given.

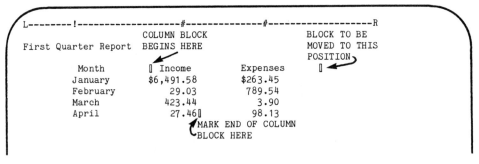

```
L--------!-------------------#--------------#-------------------R
                 COLUMN BLOCK                  BLOCK TO BE
First Quarter Report  BEGINS HERE              MOVED TO THIS
                                               POSITION
         Month      ▯ Income      Expenses     ▯
         January     $6,491.58     $263.45
         February       29.03       789.54
         March         423.44         3.90
         April          27.46▯       98.13
                          ⸕MARK END OF COLUMN
                           ⸌BLOCK HERE
```

**Figure 1**   Screen display showing the cursor placement to mark column block move.

```
L--------!-------------------#--------------#-------------------R

First Quarter Report

         Month         Expenses      Income
         January       $263.45      $6,491.58
         February       789.54         29.03
         March            3.90        423.44
         April           98.13         27.46
```

**Figure 2**   Screen display of Figure 1 after column block is moved.

### 7.4 Writing to and from Files

The next two commands allow you to move text between files. I use them quite often, although it was a while before I found out about them.

| Command | Function |
|---------|----------|
| ^KR | Read a file into current file |

**Comments.** This command may be given any time during editing. When you give the command, WordStar will ask you for the name of the file to read. You respond with the name of the file and then RETURN. WordStar will take the file you have named and insert it in the file you are editing, beginning at the cursor position. If there is any text in the file you are editing below the cursor position, it will be moved down to make room for the file you are reading, regardless of whether the INSERT is on or off. I use this command in conjunction with the next command to move text between files.

| Command | Function |
|---------|----------|
| ^KW | Write marked block to file |

**Comments.** This command can be used after you have marked a block of text, as long as the column mode is not on. When you type ^KW, WordStar will respond with

```
NAME OF FILE TO WRITE MARKED TEXT ON?
```

You type the name of the file you want the marked block written to. Suppose you have marked a block and want a copy of it written to a file named TEMP on drive A. If the file TEMP is not a new one, WordStar will display the following

```
FILE A:TEMP  EXISTS -- OVERWRITE? (Y/N):
```

To which you can respond yes by typing y, or no by typing n. If you type y, WordStar will copy the marked block onto the file you have named and delete anything that was in it previously, so be careful with this command. The block you have marked is copied to the file you have named, and also remains in the file you are editing.

**Example.** I use this command in many situations. For example, when I have set up the dot commands I am using in a file, I may write them to a file with the name DOTS if I am going to be setting up other files in the same format. That way, when I open a new file that is to have the same format, I begin by reading in the file DOTS with the ^KR command. This saves me from having to look into the old file to see what the dot commands were and then retyping them into the new file. There are many other similar situations in which I use the ^KW and ^KR commands. They are mostly situations in which I have a section of one file that I want to include in another file. I begin by marking the section and then writing it to a temporary file. Next, I call up the file I want the section written to and give the ^KR command to read the temporary file into the new file.

# Printing Programs
# for WordStar

There are a number of programs on the market that allow you to take advantage of the features on your dot-matrix printer without having to use the installation program that accompanies WordStar.

The one I use for my Epson FX-80 is called *Wsprint*. With it, my Epson printer will do almost everything my NEC letter-quality printer will do, including interpreting the dot command that changes the line height. Wsprint does not become part of your WordStar program. It remains separate. I have WordStar installed for my NEC letter-quality printer. When I want to print a file on my NEC, I use WordStar. When I want to print a file on my Epson, I use Wsprint. The program costs $39.95. There are versions of the program available for Epson MX-80 printers, as well as the C. Itoh Prowriter, and many others. When you write to place your order (as far as I know, their telephone number is unlisted), be sure to specify the make and model of your printer, as well as the diskette format you will need. It may take quite a while to get a response, so be prepared to wait. Here is their address:

Wheatland Design Laboratory
2601 Belle Crest
Lawrence, KS 66044

Another program I have used is called *Printerization*. It is also available for Epson printers and C. Itoh Prowriters, as well as the NEC 8023, the IDS Prism, and many other printers. Unlike Wsprint, this program is not separate from WordStar; rather, it is a program that actually modifies WordStar. Once you run the Printerization program, you no longer need it. With this program, you can take advantage of more features of your dot-matrix printer than you can by using the installation program that accompanies WordStar. The cost is about $35. The manufacturer's address and phone number are given below. I have called them on a number of occasions and found them to be very willing to answer my questions.

C. I. Software
1380 Garnet Ave. E149
San Diego, CA 92109
(619) 483-6384

Finally, we should mention a program named *Cartech.* I have never used this program, but I have spoken with the manufacturer and read their brochure. Like Printerization, Cartech is a program that will modify WordStar so that you can access more of the features of your dot-matrix printer. With Cartech you can print mathematical symbols and Greek characters. But the most interesting thing about this program is that, with certain computers and terminals, it will also display Greek and math characters on your screen. As of this writing, the program can cost you anywhere from $65 to almost $200, depending on what kind of system you have and how many of their features you wish to install. They have a fifty-page manual that you can purchase for $10. It may be a good idea to purchase the manual first and then, if you like what you see, purchase the program. Here is the address and phone number of the manufacturer:

Techware
1633 High Street
Eugene, OR 97401
(503) 484-0520

# B

# Installing Dot-Matrix Printers with WordStar 3.0

In this appendix we show you the way in which the WordStar installation program is used to install a dot-matrix printer. Our main goal is to install a dot-matrix printer so that it will print full-sized superscripts and subscripts one half line above or below the line of text on which they appear. The way in which this is accomplished depends on whether or not the printer can move its carriage up or down a half line, while leaving the print head in the same column.

This appendix is not intended to be a step-by-step guide for a first time installation of WordStar. You should use the information in this appendix only if you already have an installed version of WordStar; that is, a version of WordStar that was installed for you by the dealer you bought it from, or a version that you have installed yourself.

Using the installation program the way we are going to be using it here can be a frustrating experience. For that reason, you may want to consider buying a separate program that will allow you to bypass this installation procedure. Three such programs are listed in Appendix A.

As a final note, we offer this advice: Be absolutely sure you are working with a backup copy of WordStar when you do the installation procedures outlined here. Do not use your original version. Start with a new diskette, put the installation program on it, along with a copy of WordStar (including the WordStar overlay files), and then make the modifications given in this appendix. That way, if you make some mistakes, and end up with a version of WordStar that is unusable, you will not have lost anything.

## Calling up the Installation Program

Your installation program will be under the name INSTALL.COM, or WINSTALL.COM. Call it up by typing INSTALL, or WINSTALL at the A⟩ prompt. When WordStar asks you if this is a first-time installation, answer no. WordStar will then list four options for you, choose option C. When you have done so, your screen will look like this:

```
Do you want a normal first-time INSTALLation of WordStar?
(Y = yes;  N = display other options): N


        *****  WordStar INSTALLATION OPTIONS MENU  *****

A  INSTALLation of a distributed WordStar, INSTALLing WSU.COM,
   producing WS.COM, and then running the INSTALLed WordStar.

B  INSTALLation or re-INSTALLation of a WordStar COM file of your
   your choice, placing the newly INSTALLed WordStar in a file
   of your choice, and then exiting to the operating system.

C  Same a B except run the INSTALLed WordStar.

D  Modification of the INSTALLation of a WordStar COM file of
   your choice.  The modified WordStar replaces the original
   file.  The modified WordStar is then run.

PLEASE ENTER SELECTION (A, B, C, or D): C

Filename of WordStar to be INSTALLed?
```

WordStar is now asking you for the file name of WordStar that you want to install. If you have not altered the name of your WordStar program, type WS.COM, or just WS, and then press RETURN. What you will be doing is taking an already installed WordStar and making some additional modifications to it. That is why you answer the above question with WS.COM.

Next you will be asked for the name of the file you want the new version of WordStar saved under. Give a different name than the one you gave above. I use WSE.COM. That way, my old copy of WordStar will not be changed. My new copy is under the name WSE.COM, so I can test it on my printer before I rename it WS.COM.

Now when the menu of terminals comes on, simply press RETURN to leave it as it is. Then press RETURN again when WordStar asks you to verify your selection.

If you have followed the procedures shown here, the menu of printers should now be on your screen. At this point you need to consult the manual that came with your printer to see if your printer can move its carriage up or down a half line without altering the position of the print head. In the manual for the Epson FX-80, the commands that do this are called *paper feed* and *reverse paper feed*. Generally, what you are looking for are two commands. One will roll the carriage up a fraction of a line (that is move the paper down a fraction of a line) and the other will do the opposite. These commands do not permanently alter the line height. Also note that the *line feed* and *reverse line feed* commands on most printers are not the commands you are looking for. Under WordStar, a line feed (and a reverse line feed) will also return the print head to the left side of the paper. If your printer has the commands in question, then select A or C in the menu of printers, depending on whether your printer can also backspace. (If you have an Epson FX-80 printer, then select C.)

If your printer cannot move the carriage up or down a fraction of a line without returning the print head to the left side of the paper, then select I. (If you have an Epson MX-80 printer, then you are in this category.)

After you have selected the appropriate option from the menu of printers, press RETURN in response to the next questions until WordStar asks:

```
ARE THE MODIFICATIONS TO WORDSTAR NOW COMPLETE?

   IF THEY ARE ANSWER YES TO THE NEXT QUESTION.
   IF YOU WISH TO MAKE ADDITIONAL PATCHES TO WORDSTAR'S
   USER AREAS, ANSWER NO TO THE NEXT QUESTION.

OK (Y/N) :
```

Answer no, and see the following on your screen:

```
YOU MAY NOW MODIFY ANY LOCATION DESCRIBED IN THE LISTING
AT THE END OF THE USER MANUAL OR THE CUSTOMIZATION NOTES.

YOU MAY USE EITHER THE LABEL OR THE HEX ADDRESS TO SPECIFY
THE LOCATIONS YOU WISH TO CHANGE.  IF YOU USE A LABEL THEN
YOU MAY APPEND AN OFFSET TO THE LABEL (I.E. LABEL:+31).  THE
LABEL ALWAYS HAS A ":" APPENDED (LABEL:). YOU MAY SPECIFY
THE NEW VALUE ONLY AS A HEX NUMBER.  A LOCATION OF ZERO (0)
WILL CAUSE THE END OF THE MODIFICATIONS

LOCATION TO BE CHANGED (0=END) :
```

This is the point at which you begin the custom installation of your printer. How you answer this question depends on whether your printer can roll its carriage up and down a fraction of a line without returning the print head to the left side of the paper. If your printer is capable of doing this, then keep reading. If it cannot do this, then go to the section entitled "Dot-Matrix Printers That Cannot Roll the Carriage a Fraction of a Line."

## Dot-Matrix Printers That Can Roll the Carriage Up and Down a Fraction of a Line

Before we actually show the next series of responses, we need to have an overview of what we are trying to do. We are going to change the values in the locations in WordStar named ROLUP and ROLDOW. These locations will contain the codes that your printer uses to roll its carriage up or down a half line. As an example we will show the values you would use if you were installing an Epson FX-80 printer.

To instruct an Epson FX-80 printer to roll the carriage up $\frac{1}{12}$ of an inch, without moving the print head, you must send it the string ESC j 18. In the Epson manual, this sequence of commands is under the title "Reverse Paper Feed." In the manual it is described as ESC j n, where $n$ is a number between 0 and 255, that will cause the $n/216$ inch line feed. When we send the code sequence ESC j 18 to an Epson FX-80, it will cause the Epson to roll its carriage up $\frac{18}{216}$, or $\frac{1}{12}$, of an inch. If we are printing text in the normal six lines per inch, $\frac{1}{12}$ of an inch will amount to one half line. Since the installation program only accepts characters in hexadecimal, we will insert the sequence 1B 6A 12 which are the hexadecimal equivalent of ESC j 18.

Now all we need to do is put the string ESC j 18 into the location named *ROLUP*. To begin, we call up the location ROLUP, and tell WordStar how many characters are in the string that we want to place there. It will be the same with all modifications you make at specific locations in WordStar; the first thing you do is give the number of characters in the character string you are placing at the location in question.

Here we go. In response to the question about the location to be changed, type ROLUP: (including the colon) followed by RETURN. For the new value, give 3, then press RETURN. This tells WordStar the character string we are going to put at ROLUP is three characters long. WordStar will then ask for the next location to be changed. Press RETURN to get the location ROLUP+0001. (Pressing RETURN when WordStar asks you for the location to be changed automatically gets you to the next location, past the one you specified previously.) For the new value at this location, type 1B, the hexadecimal equivalent of ESC. Then press RETURN twice to get to location ROLUP+0002. At this location type 6A, the hexadecimal equivalent of j. Press RETURN twice, and you will be at location ROLUP+0003. Now type 12, the hexadecimal equivalent of the decimal number 18.

If you have followed the procedure exactly as we have indicated, your screen should look like this (the characters you typed are shown in boldface):

```
LOCATION TO BE CHANGED (O=END): ROLUP:
   ADDRESS : 06BFH    OLD VALUE: 00H    NEW VALUE: 3
LOCATION TO BE CHANGED (O=END): ROLUP+0001
   ADDRESS : 06C0H    OLD VALUE: 00H    NEW VALUE: 1B
LOCATION TO BE CHANGED (O=END): ROLUP+0002
   ADDRESS : 06C1H    OLD VALUE: 00H    NEW VALUE: 6A
LOCATION TO BE CHANGED (O=END): ROLUP+0003
   ADDRESS : 06C2H    OLD VALUE: 00H    NEW VALUE: 12
LOCATION TO BE CHANGED (O=END):
```

This completes what we want to do at the location ROLUP. If you are installing a printer other than an FX-80, then the codes you specify at ROLUP will probably be different than the ones that we have given here. Note that the maximum number of characters you can place in the location ROLUP is five, and the first of these must be the number of characters in the string that follows. So, essentially, you have a maximum of four characters in the string you insert to roll your carriage up a half line.

Next we want to change the values at the location *ROLDOW*. In response to the next location to be changed, type ROLDOW: (including the colon) followed by RETURN. The values at ROLDOW and the next three locations after it are 3, 1B, 4A, and 12. This will cause the sequence ESC J 18 to be sent to our Epson when we begin a subscript or end a superscript in our text. Here is how your screen should look when you are finished.

```
LOCATION TO BE CHANGED (O=END): ROLDOW:
   ADDRESS : 06C4H    OLD VALUE: 00H    NEW VALUE: 3
LOCATION TO BE CHANGED (O=END): ROLDOW+0001
   ADDRESS : 06C5H    OLD VALUE: 00H    NEW VALUE: 1B
LOCATION TO BE CHANGED (O=END): ROLDOW+0002
   ADDRESS : 06C6H    OLD VALUE: 00H    NEW VALUE: 4A
LOCATION TO BE CHANGED (O=END): ROLDOW+0003
   ADDRESS : 06C7H    OLD VALUE: 00H    NEW VALUE: 12
LOCATION TO BE CHANGED (O=END):
```

Now is a good time to stop and try it out. For the next location type 0 (zero) and RETURN. You will leave this part of the installation program and will be asked if the modifications to WordStar are complete. Answer yes. Your new version of WordStar will come on the screen. I suggest that you create a file that contains exponents and subscripts, and then print the file. You will find out very quickly if your installation has worked or not. If it has not worked, you may be mistaken about what your printer can and cannot do. For example, if you installed a normal line feed (the symbol LF which is 0A in hexadecimal) at ROLDOW, and a reverse line feed at ROLUP, your printer will do strange things when it encounters a superscript or subscript. These commands just do not work with WordStar because they are all accompanied by a carriage return. I have spent hours trying to install a C. Itoh printer in this manner and never had any luck whatsoever. If this is happening to you, then either install your printer according to the procedures in the next section or buy one of the print programs listed in Appendix A.

## Dot-Matrix Printers That Cannot Roll the
## Carriage a Fraction of a Line

If you cannot get your printer to roll the carriage up and down a fraction of a line by using the installation procedure outlined above, then you will have to install it as a half-line-feed printer, and then make some modifications to the location PSINIT in WordStar. Here is how it is done on an Epson MX-80 printer.

From the menu of printers in the installation program, select option I "Half-Line-Feed" printer. Now press RETURN in response to the rest of the questions until the installation program displays the following on your screen:

```
ARE THE MODIFICATIONS TO WORDSTAR NOW COMPLETE?

   IF THEY ARE ANSWER YES TO THE NEXT QUESTION.
   IF YOU WISH TO MAKE ADDITIONAL PATCHES TO WORDSTAR'S
   USER AREAS, ANSWER NO TO THE NEXT QUESTION.

OK (Y/N) : N
```

Answer no, and see the following on your screen:

```
YOU MAY NOW MODIFY ANY LOCATION DESCRIBED IN THE LISTING
AT THE END OF THE USER MANUAL OR THE CUSTOMIZATION NOTES.

YOU MAY USE EITHER THE LABEL OR THE HEX ADDRESS TO SPECIFY
THE LOCATIONS YOU WISH TO CHANGE.  IF YOU USE A LABEL THEN
YOU MAY APPEND AN OFFSET TO THE LABEL (I.E. LABEL:+31).  THE
LABEL ALWAYS HAS A ":" APPENDED (LABEL:). YOU MAY SPECIFY
THE NEW VALUE ONLY AS A HEX NUMBER.  A LOCATION OF ZERO (0)
WILL CAUSE THE END OF THE MODIFICATIONS

LOCATION TO BE CHANGED (0=END) :
```

The location we want to change is PSINIT. *PSINIT* is the location at which you begin the character string that is used to initialize your printer. That is, the character string you place there will be sent to your printer before any printing begins.

You want to modify WordStar so that the character string that begins at PSINIT will change the line spacing from six lines per inch to twelve lines per inch. On an Epson MX-80 printer, the string that sets the line spacing to twelve lines per inch is ESC A 6. Since the WordStar installation program requires these characters to be given in hexadecimal, we will place the string 1B 41 06 at the location PSINIT.

The location PSINIT should already have a one character string of 0D installed. The code 0D (the first character is the number zero) is the hexadecimal equivalent of a carriage return. It is installed at PSINIT so that the print head is returned to the left side of the paper before printing. We will install our string after it. Since our string is three characters long (remember, this is for the Epson MX-80 printer—if you are installing a different printer, the string you use may have a different number of characters) and will be installed after the character 0D that is already in PSINIT, we will first place the number 4 at PSINIT to tell WordStar how many characters are in the string. When the location PSINIT is modified for the Epson MX-80 printer, it will look like this:

```
LOCATION TO BE CHANGED (0=END): PSINIT:
    ADDRESS : 06E7H   OLD VALUE: 01H   NEW VALUE: 4
LOCATION TO BE CHANGED (0=END): PSINIT+0001
    ADDRESS : 06E8H   OLD VALUE: 0AH   NEW VALUE: 0D
LOCATION TO BE CHANGED (0=END): PSINIT+0002
    ADDRESS : 06E9H   OLD VALUE: 00H   NEW VALUE: 1B
LOCATION TO BE CHANGED (0=END): PSINIT+0003
    ADDRESS : 06EAH   OLD VALUE: 00H   NEW VALUE: 41
LOCATION TO BE CHANGED (0=END): PSINIT+0004
    ADDRESS : 06EBH   OLD VALUE: 00H   NEW VALUE: 6
```

Now your printer is set to print twelve lines per inch, which you may think is a little strange. When you selected the *I* option in the menu of printers, you told the installation program that you were using a half-line-feed printer. The installation program automatically changes WordStar so that every time you press the RETURN key while entering text, WordStar places a carriage return and *two* line feeds in your file. (You do not see them.) Therefore, when you print a file that is single-spaced, your printer will do two $\frac{1}{2}$-inch line feeds between each line. But when WordStar encounters a superscript or subscript, it will give only one $\frac{1}{2}$-inch line feed. Thus, exponents and subscripts will appear a half line above or below the line on which they occur. There is only one problem with this method of installing WordStar: If one line of text contains a subscript and the next line contains a superscript, the superscript will *not* be printed a half line above the line of text on which it occurs because there is already a character on that line, namely the subscript from the previous line.

To leave the installation program, type 0 (zero) and press RETURN in response to the question about the next location to be changed. You will leave this part of the installation program and will be asked if the modifications to WordStar are complete. Answer yes. Your new version of WordStar will come on the screen. I suggest you create a file that contains exponents and subscripts, and then print the file with your newly installed version of WordStar to find out if the modifications you have made have worked or not.

## Additional Modifications to WordStar

If your printer can produce special type styles and fonts, you can take advantage of them by using the installation program to make additional modifications to WordStar. The procedure to do so is the same as the procedure we used to modify WordStar for superscripts and subscripts. Here are the three steps we use:

1. Give the name of the location you want to change, followed by a colon. Then press RETURN.
2. Give the number of characters in the string of characters you wish to insert. Then press RETURN twice to get to the next location.
3. Type the character string, one character at a time, following each character with two RETURNs.

When you are finished with all the modifications, type 0 (zero), followed by RETURN for the next location to be changed. Then answer yes when WordStar asks if the modifications are complete.

Here is a list of the modifications I have made to WordStar in order to take advantage of some of the special features of my Epson FX-80 printer. Remember, the character strings here will only work on an Epson. If you are installing a different printer, you will have to use your printer's codes instead of the ones listed here.

I have my Epson installed so that the standard type is the ten-pitch pica. The alternate type is the twelve-pitch elite which I access during editing by typing ^PA, which places ^A in my file at the cursor position. To return to ten-pitch pica I type ^PN, placing ^N in my file.

Epson feature:   standard pica (ten-pitch) type

Code sequence as given in Epson manual:   ESC P

Equivalent code sequence in hexadecimal:   1B 50

To be installed in WordStar location:   PSTD

WordStar command to access this feature while editing:   ^PN

```
LOCATION TO BE CHANGED (0=END): PSTD:
   ADDRESS : 06BAH   OLD VALUE: 00H   NEW VALUE: 2
LOCATION TO BE CHANGED (0=END): PSTD+0001
   ADDRESS : 06BBH   OLD VALUE: 00H   NEW VALUE: 1B
LOCATION TO BE CHANGED (0=END): PSTD+0002
   ADDRESS : 06BCH   OLD VALUE: 00H   NEW VALUE: 50
LOCATION TO BE CHANGED (0=END):
```

Epson feature:   alternate elite (twelve-pitch) type

Code sequence as given in Epson manual:   ESC M

Equivalent code sequence in hexadecimal:   1B 4D

To be installed in WordStar location:   PALT

WordStar command to access this feature while editing:   ^PA

```
LOCATION TO BE CHANGED (0=END): PALT:
   ADDRESS : 06B5H   OLD VALUE: 00H   NEW VALUE: 2
LOCATION TO BE CHANGED (0=END): PALT+0001
   ADDRESS : 06B6H   OLD VALUE: 00H   NEW VALUE: 1B
LOCATION TO BE CHANGED (0=END): PALT+0002
   ADDRESS : 06B7H   OLD VALUE: 00H   NEW VALUE: 4D
LOCATION TO BE CHANGED (0=END):
```

The Epson printer can print half-size superscripts and subscripts. I have installed my Epson so that these superscripts are turned on with the command ^PQ, the subscripts are turned on by ^PW, and both are turned off by ^PE.

Epson feature:   Begin half-size superscripts

Code sequence as given in Epson manual:   ESC S 0

Equivalent code sequence in hexadecimal:   1B 53 00

To be installed in WordStar location:   USR1

WordStar command to access this feature while editing:   ^PQ

```
LOCATION TO BE CHANGED (0=END): USR1:
    ADDRESS : 06C9H   OLD VALUE: 00H   NEW VALUE: 3
LOCATION TO BE CHANGED (0=END): USR1+0001
    ADDRESS : 06CAH   OLD VALUE: 00H   NEW VALUE: 1B
LOCATION TO BE CHANGED (0=END): USR1+0002
    ADDRESS : 06CBH   OLD VALUE: 00H   NEW VALUE: 53
LOCATION TO BE CHANGED (0=END): USR1+0003
    ADDRESS : 06CCH   OLD VALUE: 00H   NEW VALUE: 0
LOCATION TO BE CHANGED (0=END):
```

Epson feature:   Begin half-size subscripts

Code sequence as given in Epson manual:   ESC S 1

Equivalent code sequence in hexadecimal:   1B 53 01

To be installed in WordStar location:   USR2

WordStar command to access this feature while editing:   ^PW

```
LOCATION TO BE CHANGED (0=END): USR2:
    ADDRESS : 06CEH   OLD VALUE: 00H   NEW VALUE: 3
LOCATION TO BE CHANGED (0=END): USR2+0001
    ADDRESS : 06CFH   OLD VALUE: 00H   NEW VALUE: 1B
LOCATION TO BE CHANGED (0=END): USR2+0002
    ADDRESS : 06D0H   OLD VALUE: 00H   NEW VALUE: 53
LOCATION TO BE CHANGED (0=END): USR2+0003
    ADDRESS : 06D1H   OLD VALUE: 00H   NEW VALUE: 1
LOCATION TO BE CHANGED (0=END):
```

Epson feature:   End half-size superscripts and subscripts

Code sequence as given in Epson manual:   ESC T

Equivalent code sequence in hexadecimal:   1B 54

To be installed in WordStar location:   USR3

WordStar command to access this feature while editing:   ^PE

```
LOCATION TO BE CHANGED (O=END): USR3:
    ADDRESS : 06D3H    OLD VALUE: 00H    NEW VALUE: 2
LOCATION TO BE CHANGED (O=END): USR3+0001
    ADDRESS : 06D4H    OLD VALUE: 00H    NEW VALUE: 1B
LOCATION TO BE CHANGED (O=END): USR3+0002
    ADDRESS : 06D5H    OLD VALUE: 00H    NEW VALUE: 54
LOCATION TO BE CHANGED (O=END):
```

Since I do not use ribbons in my printers that can print in two different colors, I use the command that would change ribbon color, ^PY, to begin and end printing in condensed type.

Epson feature:   Begin condensed type

Code sequence as given in Epson manual:   ESC SI

Equivalent code sequence in hexadecimal:   1B 0F

To be installed in WordStar location:   RIBBON

WordStar command to access this feature while editing:   ^PY

```
LOCATION TO BE CHANGED (O=END): RIBBON:
    ADDRESS : 06DDH    OLD VALUE: 00H    NEW VALUE: 2
LOCATION TO BE CHANGED (O=END): RIBBON+0001
    ADDRESS : 06DEH    OLD VALUE: 00H    NEW VALUE: 1B
LOCATION TO BE CHANGED (O=END): RIBBON+0002
    ADDRESS : 06DFH    OLD VALUE: 00H    NEW VALUE: 0F
LOCATION TO BE CHANGED (O=END):
```

Epson feature:   End condensed type

Code sequence as given in Epson manual:   DC2

Equivalent code sequence in hexadecimal:   12

To be installed in WordStar location:   RIBOFF

WordStar command to access this feature while editing:   ^PY

```
LOCATION TO BE CHANGED (O=END): RIBOFF:
    ADDRESS : 06E2H    OLD VALUE: 00H    NEW VALUE: 1
LOCATION TO BE CHANGED (O=END): RIBOFF+0001
    ADDRESS : 06E3H    OLD VALUE: 00H    NEW VALUE: 12
LOCATION TO BE CHANGED (O=END):
```

When you are finished with all the modifications you want to make, type 0 (zero) in response to the next location to be changed, followed by RETURN. WordStar will ask if the modifications are complete. Answer yes.

# Installing Dot-Matrix Printers with WordStar 3.3

In this appendix we show you how to use the installation program that accompanies version 3.3 of WordStar to install a dot-matrix printer. Our main goal is to install a dot-matrix printer so that it will print full-sized superscripts and subscripts one half line above or below the line of text on which they appear. There are four main parts to this appendix. In the first part, we show you how to call up the installation program and name the file you want to modify. In the second part, we cover installation of printers that can roll the carriage up or down a half line, while leaving the print head in the same column. The third part covers installation of printers that cannot roll the carriage up or down a fraction of a line. The fourth, and final part of this appendix, lists some additional modifications that can be made to WordStar.

The best way to use this appendix is to read completely through the section that is appropriate to your printer and then try the procedures yourself. But be aware that this appendix is not intended to be a step-by-step guide for a first time installation of WordStar. You should use the information in this appendix only if you already have an installed version of WordStar, that is, a version of WordStar that was installed for you by the dealer you bought it from, or a version that you have installed yourself.

Using the installation program the way we are going to be using it here can be a frustrating experience. For that reason you may want to consider buying a separate program that will allow you to bypass this installation procedure. We have listed three such programs in Appendix A.

As a final note, we offer this advice: Be absolutely sure you are working with a backup copy of WordStar when you follow the installation procedures outlined here. Do not use your original version. Start with a new diskette, put the installation program on it, along with a copy of WordStar (including the WordStar overlay files and the file WS.INS), and then make the modifications given in this appendix. That way, if you make some mistakes, and end up with a version of WordStar that is unusable, you will not have lost anything.

### Calling up the Installation Program

Your installation program will be under the name INSTALL.COM, or WINSTALL.COM. Call it up by typing INSTALL, or WINSTALL at the A⟩ prompt, followed by RETURN. The first thing you will see is a paragraph on copyrights, followed by a message to type any key to continue. Press any key and see the following on your screen.

```
With INSTALL you can set up your terminal and printer
for use with MicroPro programs.  You can also change
certain features of the program with INSTALL

    Would you like to continue?
                    Enter Y or <RETURN> for Yes.
                    Enter N for No.
```

Type Y or press RETURN to see the following message displayed on your screen.

```
        Which MicroPro product would you like to Install?
        Enter - WS for WordStar
              - WM for WordMaster
              - DS for DataStar
              - RS for ReportStar
        then press <RETURN>.

Product?
```

Type WS and press the RETURN key. Your screen will then fill with some general information about using the installation program. After you have read this information, press RETURN to see the following on your screen.

```
Enter the disk drive name (a letter followed by a colon,
B:) where WordStar files will be located while you run
INSTALL: then press <RETURN>.
```

If you have enough room on your diskettes, it is easiest to have all the files on the diskette in drive A. If so, type A: (including the colon) followed by RETURN in response to the above question. If your diskettes will not hold the installation program and the WordStar files at the same time, put the installation program on the diskette in drive A and the WordStar files on the diskette in drive B and type B: followed by RETURN in response to the above question.

Next you will be asked for the name of the WordStar file you are going to install and the name you want it saved under when you are finished installing it. The name of the file you are going to install is WS.COM. (Remember, we are assuming you are working with an already installed version of WordStar.) After you are finished making the modifications to it, you will save it under another name. The name we are using here is WSE.COM. If you want to use another name, type that name instead of WSE.COM. Here is how your screen will look when you have answered these questions. The boldface represents your responses.

```
The uninstalled WordStar program is normally contained in WSU.COM.
If you are reinstalling WordStar or have previously renamed
the file, enter the new name below; otherwise press <RETURN>.

    NAME OF FILE TO INSTALL, OR <RETURN> for A:WSU.COM WS RETURN


    File to install is : WS.COM



When you are finished running this program, you will have an
installed version of WordStar in a new file on the logged
disk drive.  It will be called A:WS.COM. If you wish to name the
file something else, enter the name below. Otherwise press
<RETURN>. To change the name, enter up to eight letters or
numbers. The extension .COM will automatically be added to any
name.

    Enter name of file for installed WordStar, or <RETURN> for A:WS.COM WSE RETURN
```

Now the installation program will ask you to confirm your selections. If the selections you have made are correct, press RETURN until the installation menu appears on the screen. It will look like this:

```
      *****  INSTALLATION MENU  *****

If you are installing a new copy of WordStar, you must select
letter A to install your terminal, then letter C to install
your printer. If your terminal is not listed on the Menu of
Terminals, return to this menu and select letter B. If your
printer is not listed on the Menu of Printers, return to this
menu and select letter D. If you want to change a particular
WordStar feature, choose letter D.


A  Menu of Terminals
B  Custom Installation of Terminals

C  Menu of Printers
D  Custom Installation of Printers

E  Menu of WordStar Features
F  Operating System Considerations

X  Exit from INSTALL

   Enter the letter of your choice (A/B/C/D/E/F/X). C
```

From the installation menu, type C to get the menu of printers on your screen. It will look like this:

```
      *****  STANDARD PRINTER TYPES  *****

Select the letter of your printer from the list below.
This is menu  #1 of 2; to view another menu press the
appropriate number.

A C. Itoh/TEC Starwriter/F10   G Epson MX80/100-no Graftrax
B Centronics 353               H Half line feed printer
C Centronics 739               I IBM Parallel printer
D Diablo 630                   J MPI 88G/99G
E Diablo/Xerox 1610/1620       K NEC 8023A matrix printer
F Diablo/Xerox 1640/1650       L NEC Spinwriter 3550

   Enter the letter of your choice,
   or enter the appropriate menu number,
   or press <RETURN> to leave unchanged.
```

At this point you need to consult the manual that came with your printer to see if your printer can move its carriage up or down a half line without altering the position of the print head. In the manual for the Epson FX-80, the commands that do this are called *paper feed* and *reverse paper feed.* Generally, what you are looking for are two commands, one of which will roll the carriage up a fraction of a line and the other which will do the opposite. These commands do not permanently alter the line height. Also note that the *line feed* and *reverse line feed* commands on most printers are not the commands you are looking for. Under WordStar, a line feed (and a reverse line feed) will also return the print head to the left side of the paper. If your printer does not have the commands in question, then type H from the menu of printers to select a half-line-feed printer, and then skip to the section entitled "Dot-Matrix Printers That Cannot Roll the Carriage a Fraction of a Line" later in this appendix (if you have an Epson MX-80 printer, you are in this category).

## Dot-Matrix Printers That Can Roll the Carriage Up and Down a Fraction of a Line

If your printer is capable of rolling the carriage up and down a fraction of a line, then type 2 to get the second menu of printers. It looks like this:

```
     *****  STANDARD PRINTER TYPES  *****

Select the letter of your printer from the list below.
This is menu  #2 of 2; to view another menu press the
appropriate number.

A NEC Spinwriter specialty   E TI 810/820
B Okidata ML84A              F backspacing standard
C Olympia ESW-102            G standard printer
D Qume Sprint 5-9/45-11I+

    Enter the letter of your choice,
    or enter the appropriate menu number,
    or press <RETURN> to leave unchanged.
```

From this menu, type F if your printer can also backspace or G if it cannot. (If you have an Epson FX-80 printer, then select F.)

After you have selected the appropriate option from the menu of printers, the installation program will ask you to confirm your selection. Then you will be asked some questions about communications protocol and your printer driver. Leave these as they are by pressing RETURN as your response. (Remember, we are assuming that you are making modifications to an already installed WordStar. So it shouldn't be necessary for you to change the communications protocol or printer driver.)

When the installation menu comes back on the screen, select option D for custom installation of printers. Your screen will then fill with information about the printer installation menu. When you have read the information, press RETURN to get to the printer installation menu. This is what it looks like:

```
      *****   PRINTER INSTALLATION MENU   *******

A  Automatic installation for Specialty printers
B  Automatic installation for Standard printers

All printers                      Specialty printers only

C  Printer name                   I  Ribbon selection
D  Initialization                 J  Vertical motion
E  Overprinting                   K  Horizontal motion
F  Boldfacing                     L  Print modes
G  Protocol menu                  M  Phantom characters
H  Driver menu

Standary printers only            Optional

N  Return / line feed             O  User-defined functions
                                  P  Carriage roll
                                  Q  Character pitch
X  Exit to INSTALLATION menu

   Enter the letter of your choice (A-Q/X).
```

Before we actually show the responses you will give next, let's explain what we are trying to do. We are going to give WordStar the code sequences necessary to roll the printer carriage up and down a fraction of a line. To do so we must first type P from the printer installation menu to get into the locations in WordStar that control the carriage roll. Once we are in the appropriate location in the installation program, we type in the code sequence that is to be sent to our printer. As an example of how to proceed with this, we will show the code sequences you would use if you were installing an Epson FX-80 printer. To instruct an Epson FX-80 printer to roll the carriage up $\frac{1}{12}$ of an inch, without moving the print head, you must send it the string ESC j 18. In the Epson manual, this sequence of commands is under the title "Reverse Paper Feed." In the manual it is described as ESC j n, where $n$ is a number between 0 and 255, that will cause an $n/216$ inch line feed in the opposite direction from a normal line feed. When we use 18 for $n$, we are telling our Epson printer to roll the carriage up $\frac{18}{216}$, or $\frac{1}{12}$, of an inch. If we are using the normal six lines per inch when printing a file, a carriage roll of ½ of an inch will amount to a half line.

To put the string ESC j 18 into the appropriate location in WordStar, type P from the printer installation menu to select the carriage roll option. After you have done so, the installation program will give you some information about that option and tell you the code sequence that is currently contained there. This is what it looks like on your screen:

```
              Roll up carriage

Some WordStar features, such as superscripting, require that
the carriage roll up a partial line. Check your printer
manual for the special characters required to roll the
carriage up a partial line. What sequence of characters
should be sent to the printer at "^PT" in your text?

Roll up carriage function code sequence is currently: (empty)



     Enter "C" to change,
     or press <RETURN> to leave unchanged.
```

Since you are going to change the code sequence, type C to get the following on your screen:

```
You can enter a value in ASCII, decimal, or hexadecimal
codes. Precede each entry with these prefixes:

ASCII          :   (:^A enters ASCII ^A, a single value)
Hexadecimal    ,   (,41 enters hexadecimal 41)
Decimal        #   (#61 enters decimal 61)

To enter a sequence of charcters, enter each one separately,
followed by <RETURN>.

Press <RETURN> to leave a value unchanged.
Enter a period (.) and press <RETURN> to terminate a sequence
     and to eliminate all subsequent values.

These special characters require hexadecimal input:
<RETURN> (^M)              ,0D
Period (.)                 ,2E
^H (backspace: ^H)         ,08

Maximum entries for roll up carriage function is 4

Current    New
Value      Value
00h
```

As you can see from the information on your screen, you have a choice of three different ways in which you can enter the characters in your string. You can enter them in ASCII, decimal, or hexadecimal. Since the installation program will ask you to confirm your selection by showing it to you in hexadecimal, we will enter our code sequences in hexadecimal also. If you are not sure of some of the hexadecimal equivalents of the characters in the string you are going to enter, you can look them up in Appendix D.

Here is how you alter the roll carriage up function for an Epson FX-80 printer. For the first new value, type ,1B (including the comma), the hexadecimal equivalent of ESC. Then press RETURN and type ,6A (again, including the comma) which is the hexadecimal equivalent of j. Press RETURN and type ,12 which is hexadecimal equivalent for the number 18. Finally, press RETURN two more times, and you will be finished with the roll up function.

If you have followed the procedure exactly as we have indicated, the bottom of your screen should look like this:

```
Current    New
Value      Value
00h        ,1B
00h        ,6A
00h        ,12
00h        00h ... (unchanged)


Roll up carriage function code sequence is now : 1Bh 6Ah 12h 0h

    If this is correct, enter Y or <RETURN>. If not, enter N.
```

If you have made a mistake, or would like to change the code sequence, type N and you will have the opportunity to do it again. Otherwise, press RETURN, and the installation program will display a message about the roll down carriage function. Type C to change it from its current value.

For an Epson FX-80 printer, the code sequence we want at this location is ESC J 18. (In the Epson manual it is referred to as the *paper feed* option.) Here is how the bottom of your screen will look when you have placed the hexadecimal equivalent of these characters in the roll down carriage location. (The code 4A is the hexadecimal equivalent of J.)

```
Maximum entries for roll down carriage function is 4.


Current      New
Value        Value
00h          ,1B
00h          ,4A
00h          ,12
00h          00h ... (unchanged)



Roll down carriage function code sequence is now : 1Bh 4Ah 12h 0h
```

This completes what we want to do at the carriage roll location in the installation program. If you are installing a printer other than an FX-80, then the codes you specify will probably be different than the ones we have given here. Note that the maximum number of characters you can place in the carriage roll location is four. So if your printer requires more characters than this to roll the carriage up or down a fraction of a line, you will not be able to do what we have done here.

Now is a good time to stop and try out the modifications you have made. To leave the installation program, type X's until you arrive at the exit options menu. The installation program will then show you the main choices you have made and ask you what you want to do next. The bottom of your screen will look like this:

```
        *****  EXIT OPTIONS MENU  *****

A  Save the changes made during the INSTALL session
B  Quit this session of INSTALL without saving changes
C  Change any of your choices / Remain in INSTALL

   ENTER THE LETTER OF YOUR CHOICE (A/B/C).
```

To save the modifications you have made type A. Your modified version of WordStar is called WSE.COM. To call it up, type WSE at the A) prompt.

I suggest you create a file that contains exponents and subscripts and then print the file with your newly installed version of WordStar to find out if your modifications have worked or not. If it has not worked, you may be mistaken about what your printer can and cannot do. For example, if you installed a normal line feed (the symbol LF, which is 0A in hexadecimal) at roll down carriage, and a reverse line feed at roll up carriage, your printer will do strange things when it encounters a superscript or subscript. These commands just do not work with WordStar because they are all accompanied by a carriage return. I have spent hours trying to install a C. Itoh printer in this manner and never had any luck whatsoever. If this is happening to you, then either install your printer according to the procedures in the next section or buy one of the print programs listed in Appendix A.

## Dot-Matrix Printers That Cannot Roll the Carriage a Fraction of a Line

If you cannot get your printer to roll the carriage up and down a fraction of a line by using the installation procedure outlined above, you will have to install it as a half-line-feed printer and then make some modifications to the initialization function. Here is how it is done on an Epson MX-80 printer.

From the installation menu, type C to get a menu of printers. From the menu of printers, type H to select a half-line-feed printer option. After you have selected the half-line-feed printer option, the installation program will ask you to confirm your selection. Then you will be asked some questions about communications protocol and your printer driver. Leave these as they are by pressing RETURN as your response. (Remember, we are assuming that you are making modifications to an already installed WordStar. So it shouldn't be necessary for you to change the communications protocol or printer driver.)

When the installation menu comes back on the screen, select option D for custom installation of printers. Your screen will then fill with some information about this menu. When you have read the information press RETURN to get to the printer installation menu. Here is what it looks like:

```
        *****   PRINTER INSTALLATION MENU   *******
          . . . . .                          . . . . . . .
A  Automatic installation for Specialty printers
B  Automatic installation for Standard printers

All printers                    Specialty printers only

C  Printer name                 I  Ribbon selection
D  Initialization               J  Vertical motion
E  Overprinting                 K  Horizontal motion
F  Boldfacing                   L  Print modes
G  Protocol memu                M  Phantom characters
H  Driver menu

Standary printers only          Optional

N  Return / line feed           O  User-defined functions
                                P  Carriage roll
                                Q  Character pitch
X  Exit to INSTALLATION menu

   Enter the letter of your choice (A-Q/X).
```

We are going to alter the code sequence that is sent to your printer just before it begins printing. This code sequence is accessed from the initialization by typing D from the printer installation menu. Type D and see the following displayed on your screen:

```
                  Printer initialization

This is the sequence transmitted to the printer at the start
of printing.

Printer initialization function code sequence is currently: Dh


    Enter "C" to change,
    or press <RETURN> to leave unchanged.
```

Since we want to alter the code sequence, type C. When you do so, your screen will look like this:

```
You can enter a value in ASCII, decimal, or hexadecimal
codes. Precede each entry with these prefixes:

ASCII          :    (:^A enters ASCII ^A, a single value)
Hexadecimal    ,    (,41 enters hexadecimal 41)
Decimal        #    (#61 enters decimal 61)

To enter a sequence of charcters, enter each one separately,
followed by <RETURN>.

Press <RETURN> to leave a value unchanged.
Enter a period (.) and press <RETURN> to terminate a sequence
    and to eliminate all subsequent values.

These special characters require hexadecimal input:
<RETURN> (^M)              ,0D
Period (.)                ,2E
^H (backspace: ^H)        ,08

Maximum entries for printer initialization function is 16.

Current    New
Value      Value
0Dh
```

As you can see from the information on your screen, you have a choice of three different ways in which you can enter the characters in your string. You can enter them in ASCII, decimal, or hexadecimal. Since the installation program will ask you to confirm your selection by showing it to you in hexadecimal, we will enter our code sequences in hexadecimal also. If you are not sure of some of the hexadecimal equivalents of the characters in the string you are going to enter, you can look them up in Appendix D.

You want to modify WordStar so that the code sequence sent to your printer just before it begins printing will change the line spacing from six lines per inch to twelve lines per inch. On an Epson MX-80 printer, the code sequence that sets the line spacing to twelve lines per inch is ESC A 6. (If you are installing a different printer, you will use a different code sequence.) The hexadecimal equivalent of ESC A 6 is 1B 41 06.

Note that the current value of the initialization string is 0D (the *h* following it stands for hexadecimal.) The code 0D (the first character is the number zero) is the hexadecimal equivalent of a carriage return. It is there so that the print head is returned to the left side of the paper just before printing. Since we want to leave the 0D where it is and install our code sequence after it, press RETURN to leave it unchanged. Then type ,1B (including the comma) followed by RETURN, then ,41 (again, include the comma) followed by RETURN. And finally, type ,6 and then press

RETURN. If you have followed the instructions so far, the bottom of your screen should look like this:

```
Current    New
Value      Value
0Dh        0Dh ... (unchanged)
00h        ,1B
00h        ,41
00h        ,6
00h
```

To terminate this part of the installation process, type a period and then press RETURN. You will then be asked to verify your code sequence. It looks like this:

```
Printer initialization function code sequence is not : Dh 1Bh 41h 6h

    If this is correct, enter Y or <RETURN>. If not, enter N.
```

If you have made a mistake you can go through the procedure again by typing N. If your code sequence is correct, type Y or press RETURN. The installation program will then ask you for the code sequence you want to place at the printer deinitialization location. Just press RETURN until you get back to the installation menu.

Your printer is now set to print twelve lines per inch, which you may think is a little strange. When you selected the H option on the menu of printers, you told the installation program that you were using a half-line-feed printer. The installation program automatically changes WordStar so that every time you press the RETURN key while entering text, WordStar places a carriage return and *two* line feeds in your file. (You do not see them.) Therefore, when you print a file that is single-spaced, your printer will do two $\frac{1}{2}$-inch line feeds between each line. But when WordStar encounters a superscript or subscript, it will give only one $\frac{1}{2}$-inch line feed. Thus exponents and subscripts will appear a half line above or below the line on which they occur. There is only one problem with this method of installing WordStar: If one line of text contains a subscript and the next line contains a superscript, the superscript will *not* be printed a half line above the line of text on which it occurs because there is already a character on that line, namely the subscript from the previous line.

To leave the installation program, type X's until you arrive at the exit options menu. The installation program will then show you the main choices you have made and ask you what you want to do next. The bottom of your screen will look like this:

```
      *****  EXIT OPTIONS MENU  *****

A  Save the changes made during the INSTALL session
B  Quit this session of INSTALL without saving changes
C  Change any of your choices / Remain in INSTALL

   ENTER THE LETTER OF YOUR CHOICE (A/B/C).
```

If you are ready to try out your new version of WordStar, type A. Your modified version of WordStar is under the name WSE.COM. To call it up, type WSE followed by RETURN at the A⟩ prompt.

I suggest you create a file that contains exponents and subscripts and then print the file with your newly installed version of WordStar to find out if the modifications you have made have worked or not.

### Additional Modification to WordStar

If your printer can produce special type styles and fonts, you can take advantage of them by using the installation program to make additional modifications to WordStar.

The procedure to do so is the same as the procedure we used to modify WordStar for superscripts and subscripts. From the installation menu press D for custom installation of printers. From the printer installation menu select the appropriate option and then type in your code sequence.

Here is a list of the modifications I have made to WordStar in order to take advantage of some of the special features of my Epson FX-80 printer. Remember, the character strings here will only work on an Epson. If you are installing a different printer, you will have to use your printers codes instead of the ones listed here.

I have my Epson installed so that the standard type is the ten-pitch pica. The alternate type is the twelve-pitch elite which I access during the editing by typing ^PA, which places ^A in my file at the cursor position. To return to ten-pitch pica, I type ^PN, placing ^N in my file.

Epson feature:   Alternate elite (twelve-pitch) type
Code sequence as given in Epson manual:   ESC M
Equivalent code sequence in hexadecimal:   1B 4D
Option to select from printer installation menu:   Q character pitch
WordStar command to access this feature while editing:   ^PA

**Comments.**   Install your code sequence under *alternate character pitch,* which is the first function you will be allowed to change. After you have finished with that, the installation program will ask you if you want to alter the code for *standard character pitch.* Here is the code sequence to place there.

Epson feature:   Standard pica (ten-pitch) type
Code sequence as given in Epson manual:   ESC P
Equivalent code sequence in hexadecimal:   1B 50
Option to select from printer installation menu:   Q character pitch
WordStar command to access this feature while editing:   ^PN

The Epson printer can print half-size superscripts and subscripts. I have installed my Epson so that these superscripts are turned on with the command ^PQ, the subscripts are turned on by ^PW, and both are turned off by ^PE.

Epson feature:   Begin half-size superscripts
Code sequence as given in Epson manual:   ESC S 0
Equivalent code sequence in hexadecimal:   1B 53 00
Option to select from printer installation menu:   O user-defined functions
WordStar command to access this feature while editing:   ^PQ

**Comments.**   Install the code sequence to begin half-size superscripts at the user function 1.

Epson feature:   Begin half-size subscripts
Code sequence as given in Epson manual:   ESC S 1
Equivalent code sequence in hexadecimal:   1B 53 01
Option to select from printer installation menu:   O user-defined functions
WordStar command to access this feature while editing:   ^PW

**Comments.**   Install the code to begin half-size subscripts at the user function 2.

Epson feature:   End half-size superscripts and subscripts
Code sequence as given in Epson manual:   ESC T
Equivalent code sequence in hexadecimal:   1B 54

Option to select from printer installation menu:   O user-defined functions
WordStar command to access this feature while editing:   ^PE

**Comments.**   Install the code to end half-size superscripts and subscripts at the user function 3.

Since I do not use ribbons in my printers that can print in two different colors, I use the command that would change ribbon color, ^PY, to begin and end printing in condensed type.

Epson feature:   Begin condensed type

Code sequence as given in Epson manual:   ESC SI

Equivalent code sequence in hexadecimal:   1B 0F

Option to select from printer installation menu:   I ribbon selection

WordStar command to access this feature while editing:   ^PY

**Comments.**   The code sequence to begin condensed type should be entered first. Then the code sequence to end condensed type should be entered under standard ribbon selection. The installation program will automatically ask you for this second code sequence.

Epson feature:   End condensed type

Code sequence as given in Epson manual:   DC2

Equivalent code sequence in hexadecimal:   12

Option to select from printer installation menu:   I ribbon selection

WordStar command to access this feature while editing:   ^PY

To leave the installation program, type X's until you arrive at the exit options menu. From the exit options menu, type A to save your changes.

# D

# ASCII Character Codes and Hexadecimal Equivalents

| ASCII Character | Hexadecimal Equivalent | ASCII Character | Hexadecimal Equivalent | ASCII Character | Hexadecimal Equivalent |
|---|---|---|---|---|---|
| NUL | 00 | + | 2B | U | 55 |
| SOH | 01 | , | 2C | V | 56 |
| STX | 02 | − | 2D | W | 57 |
| ETX | 03 | . | 2E | X | 58 |
| EOT | 04 | / | 2F | Y | 59 |
| ENQ | 05 | | | Z | 5A |
| ACK | 06 | 0 | 30 | [ | 5B |
| BEL | 07 | 1 | 31 | \ | 5C |
| BS | 08 | 2 | 32 | ] | 5D |
| HT | 09 | 3 | 33 | ∧ | 5E |
| LF | 0A | 4 | 34 | | 5F |
| VT | 0B | 5 | 35 | − | |
| FF | 0C | 6 | 36 | | |
| CR | 0D | 7 | 37 | ` | 60 |
| SO | 0E | 8 | 38 | a | 61 |
| SI | 0F | 9 | 39 | b | 62 |
| | | : | 3A | c | 63 |
| DLE | 10 | ; | 3B | d | 64 |
| DC1 | 11 | < | 3C | e | 65 |
| DC2 | 12 | = | 3D | f | 66 |
| DC3 | 13 | > | 3E | g | 67 |
| DC4 | 14 | ? | 3F | h | 68 |
| NAK | 15 | | | i | 69 |
| SYN | 16 | space | 40 | j | 6A |
| ETB | 17 | A | 41 | k | 6B |
| CAN | 18 | B | 42 | l | 6C |
| EM | 19 | C | 43 | m | 6D |
| SUB | 1A | D | 44 | n | 6E |
| ESC | 1B | E | 45 | o | 6F |
| FS | 1C | F | 46 | | |
| GS | 1D | G | 47 | p | 70 |
| RS | 1E | H | 48 | q | 71 |
| US | 1F | I | 49 | r | 72 |
| | | J | 4A | s | 73 |
| SP | 20 | K | 4B | t | 74 |
| ! | 21 | L | 4C | u | 75 |
| " | 22 | M | 4D | v | 76 |
| # | 23 | N | 4E | w | 77 |
| $ | 24 | O | 4F | x | 78 |
| % | 25 | | | y | 79 |
| & | 26 | P | 50 | z | 7A |
| ' | 27 | Q | 51 | { | 7B |
| ( | 28 | R | 52 | | | 7C |
| ) | 29 | S | 53 | } | 7D |
| * | 2A | T | 54 | ~ | 7E |
| | | | | DEL | 7F |

# Glossary

This glossary contains definitions for word processing terms and phrases found in this book, as well as definitions for other common terms associated with computers.

**ASCII:** The acronym for American Standard Code for Information Interchange. It is the code by which the letters, numbers, and other characters on your keyboard are assigned numerical values within your computer.

**auto-repeat:** A special feature on some keyboards by which keys that are held down for half a second or so will begin to repeat automatically.

**backup file:** A copy of a file. WordStar automatically creates a backup file of every file saved, giving the backup file the extension .BAK. It is always a good idea to back up your files by copying them onto another diskette. That way, if something happens to the diskette you use for editing, you still have copies of your files on another diskette.

**bidirectional printer:** A printer that can print bidirectionally, from right to left as well as from left to right.

**bit:** A *binary digit,* which is either a 0 or a 1. It is the smallest unit of information in a computer.

**block:** In word processing, a section of text ranging in length from one character to many pages.

**boot:** To copy the operating system from your diskette to your computer's memory. On some systems this is done automatically when the diskette is placed in the disk drive. On other systems, a RESET button is pushed, or a sequence of characters is typed from the keyboard.

**buffer:** The part of your computer's memory that is set aside to hold information that is to be processed. Some printers also have a buffer that holds incoming data until it is ready to be printed.

**byte:** A group of adjacent bits. On an eight-bit computer, one byte is made up of eight bits. On a sixteen-bit computer, one byte is made up of sixteen bits. Each character you type from your keyboard is stored in the computer as a single byte.

**character:** Any letter, number, or other symbol found on your keyboard.

**column:** In word processing, the horizontal position on the screen.

**command:** In word processing, a key stroke or series of key strokes that you use to give instructions to your word processing program. In WordStar, commands are usually given with the aid of the CONTROL key or the ESCAPE key, but they can also be given from the menu. For example, during editing, when you type ^S, you are telling the computer to move the cursor right one space. That is, you are giving a command to the computer.

**control character:** A character (or characters) that you place in a file to control a printer or other piece of external equipment. For instance, with WordStar, when you want a word printed in boldface type, you place the control characters ^B before and after it, by typing ^PB, from your keyboard. The symbol ^ represents holding down the CONTROL key on your keyboard.

**CONTROL key:** The key on your computer keyboard that is usually labled CTRL, CNTL, or ALT or marked with an up arrow (↑). In this book it is symbolized by ^. In other books it may be symbolized by an up arrow. The CONTROL key works in the same general manner as the SHIFT key, in that it gives another meaning to the characters you type while it is held down.

**CP/M:** The acronym for Control Program for Microcomputers or Control Program Monitor. It is a computer operating system, which means it is the program that controls all the other programs that you run on your computer, including WordStar.

**CRT:** The acronym for cathode ray tube. It is usually taken to mean both the screen and the unit it is housed in.

**cursor:** The small rectangle on your screen that indicates where the next character you type will be placed when you are word processing. It may or may not blink, and it is sometimes an underline symbol rather than a rectangle.

**daisy-wheel printer:** A printer that prints characters by striking a daisy wheel. The daisy wheel itself is a round plastic wheel that has letters, numbers, and other characters around its circumference.

**decimal tab:** A tab stop around which the decimal point in a number is automatically aligned.

**default value:** The original setting or value in a command. For instance, when you call up WordStar, the right margin is already set at column 65. We say 65 is the default value for the right margin.

**directory:** A list of the names of the files on a diskette.

**disk (diskette):** A round plastic disk coated with material that can hold magnetic information. It has a square cardboard cover that is not removable. When the disk is placed in the disk drive, it will rotate (spin) within the cardboard covering.

**disk drive:** The part of your computer into which you place your diskettes. It contains a read-write head that puts information onto and copies information off of the diskettes placed inside it.

**diskette:** See *disk.*

**displayed equation:** An equation that is centered on a separate line from the text around it.

**document:** In word processing, any file you have created using your word processor.

**DOS:** The acronym for disk operating system. See *operating system.*

**dot command:** In WordStar, a command that begins with a period (dot). The dot must be in column one, and the letters and numbers that follow the dot specify what the command is to do.

**dot-matrix printer:** A printer that places characters on paper by forming them with an array of dots. The print head in a dot-matrix printer contains small pins that strike the ribbon in various combinations to form the characters that are printed.

**ESC, or ESCAPE, key:** A key on your keyboard. The way in which it functions depends on the program you are running. It is not used very often with Word-Star. If you give the command ^U to interrupt a previously given command, WordStar will ask you to press the ESCAPE key.

**exit:** With computers, to leave a program and return to the operating system. That is, control of the computer is taken away from the program that is running and given back to the operating system. The WordStar command ^KX will save the file you are working on and then exit from WordStar to take you back to your operating system.

**exponent:** A superscripted number or letter. See *superscript.*

**file:** In word processing, the place where the information you type on the keyboard is stored. A file can contain anywhere from one character to hundreds of pages of text.

**file name:** The name you give to a file you are creating or editing. In WordStar, a file name has two parts that are separated by a period. The first part can consist of up to eight letters and numbers, followed by a period if there is to be a second part to the name. The second part, called the file name extension, can consist of up to three letters and numbers. It is best to avoid using asterisks and question marks anywhere in a file name. Also, in file name extensions do not use BAK,

COM, ASM, BAS, OVR, HEX, or any other extension that is commonly used by word processors and computers.

**flag:** With WordStar, a symbol that appears in the last column on your screen. For example, if you have a line of text that goes past the last column on your screen, WordStar will place a + in the last column to indicate that the line extends to the right of the screen. In this case, the + is called a flag.

**floppy disk or floppy:** Same as a disk or diskette. See *disk*.

**format:** In word processing, the way in which text is arranged on the screen or on the printout. With computers in general, format can mean the way in which information is stored on a diskette, as in IBM 8-inch standard format. It can also mean the process by which you prepare a diskette to store information, as when you format a diskette.

**function key:** A key on the keyboard that has a special meaning. On the IBM Personal Computer, there are ten function keys on the left side of the keyboard. The function of each one depends on the program you are running.

**hard copy:** The printout that you get when you print a file on your printer.

**header:** The text that appears at the top of a page but is separate from the text on that page. It may include the chapter or section numbers, as well as the page number, among other things.

**horizontal scrolling:** The process of moving the text on the screen to the left so that lines running past column 80 can be seen.

**INSERT ON:** With WordStar, the mode that allows the text you type on your keyboard to be inserted on the screen at the cursor position.

**installation program:** A program that is used to set up other programs so that they will run correctly on the equipment you have. The installation program that accompanies WordStar is the program used to tell WordStar what type of terminal and printer you will be using. It also allows you to alter some of the codes that WordStar sends to your equipment.

**I/O:** The acronym stands for input/output. It usually refers to the parallel and serial ports on the back of your computer.

**justification:** The placement of lines of text on the screen so that they begin or end at the margin. If text is right justified, then the last nonblank character on the line is on the right margin. If text is right justified, then the right margin is straight.

**letter-quality printer:** A printer that gives printouts that look like they were printed on a typewriter. The characters are printed by the print head striking the characters on a daisy wheel or thimble.

**line feed:** The process in which the printer moves its carriage up one line without returning the print head to the right margin.

**logged disk:** The disk or disk drive that is currently being used.

**memory:** The part of your computer into which your operating system and programs are placed in order to run. Memory does not refer to the amount of space on your diskettes.

**menu:** A list of options or commands available for your use. Menus are usually displayed on the screen.

**microjustification:** The system WordStar uses to align text at the right margin. It does so by placing small spaces between the words on the line.

**operating system:** The program that is used to run the other programs on your computer.

**overstrike:** One character printed on the same space as another.

**page break:** With WordStar, the line of dashes ending with a P in the far right column of the screen. This shows where one page will end and the next one will begin when the file is printed.

**pitch:** The width of the characters being printed on your printer. The standard pitches are twelve pitch, which gives twelve characters per inch on the printout, and ten pitch, which gives ten characters per inch on the printout.

**port:** A place on your computer where external equipment can be connected, for instance, the place where the cable from your printer is attached.

**printout:** The printed record you get when you print a file on your printer.

**prompt:** In word processing, a question or symbol that asks for a response from you. The symbol A⟩ is called the CP/M prompt. It is what the CP/M operating system puts on the screen when it is ready to accept input from you.

**proportional spacing:** Spacing in which the characters that are printed on your printer take up varying amounts of space (true proportional spacing). Generally, capital letters will take up more space than lowercase letters. The letter $i$ will take up less space than the letter $w$. The microjustification that WordStar produces on its printouts is not true proportional spacing.

**ragged left margin:** A left margin that has not been aligned by left justification.

**ragged right margin:** A right margin that has not been aligned by right justification.

**RETURN key:** The key on your keyboard labeled RETURN, RET, ENTER, or something similar. When pressed during word processing, it will move the cursor down one line and to the left side of the screen.

**reverse video:** A display in which the characters on your screen are light and the background is dark. It is the reverse of the way that letters are usually displayed on the screen.

**saving a file:** In word processing, telling the computer to copy the file from its memory to the diskette. With WordStar, this can be done by typing $\wedge$KD while editing. A file is not saved on your diskette until you tell the computer to save it.

**scrolling:** The process of moving through a file by having the contents of the screen move up, down, left, or right.

**soft hyphen:** A hyphen that will print only when it appears at the end of a line. While re-forming paragraphs, WordStar will ask if you want to hyphenate certain words. If you choose to do so, a soft hyphen will be placed in the position that you specify.

**software:** Generally, the programs that you run on your computer. WordStar is software, as opposed to your computer itself, which is hardware.

**subscript:** A subscripted character that is printed a half line below the other characters on the line. For example, the 2 in the formula $H_2O$ is a subscript.

**superscript:** A superscripted character that is printed a half line above the other characters on the line. For example, the 3 in the equation $x^3 = 2$ is a superscript.

**thimble:** The element that is used by an NEC Spinwriter letter-quality printer to print characters on paper.

**toggle command:** A command that can be in one of two states, ON or OFF. The INSERT mode in WordStar is a toggle command. Typing $\wedge$V when the insert is on will turn it off. Likewise, typing $\wedge$V when the insert is off will turn it on.

**word wrap:** The WordStar feature that allows you to type a paragraph without pressing the RETURN key at the end of each line. It automatically wraps words that are too long for one line onto the next line.

# Subject Index

*A separate command index follows this subject index.*

Aligning:
  equations, 45–48
  fractions, 83–86
Arrow keys, 7
ASCII (American Standard Code for
  Information Interchange) code, 128–
  129

Backups:
  of files, 6
  of program disks, 1
.BAK file extension, 6
Bidirectional printing, 73
Block operations, 12–13, 93–96
  menu for, 19
  to write to and from files, 97–98
Boldfacing, 37–39

Cartech (program), 100
Centering of equations, 45–48
Character sets for superscripts, 51–53
Characters:
  ASCII code for, 128–129
  finding, 88–90
  and replacing, 90–93
  programs to assist printing of, 100
  special (*see* Special characters)
  as subscripts, 54–56
  as superscripts, 48–53
  width of, 60–62
Color on ribbons, 43
Column mode, 95–96
Commands:
  for block operations, 12–13, 93–96

Commands (*Cont.*):
  centering, 46
  to change fonts, 51–52
  to change paper roll for superscripts
    and subscripts, 57
  for cursor movement and scrolling, 6–9
  for deleting text, 11–12
  formatting, 21–33
  to hide control characters, 50
  for insert mode, 9–10
  listed on menus, 17–20
  in opening menu, 3, 13–17
  printer, in installation procedures, 103,
    115–116
  printing, 34–44
  for re-forming paragraphs, 10–11
  to save files, 5
  for search and replace operations, 88–
    93
  for subscript printing, 54–56
  for superscript printing, 48–49
  for writing to and from files, 97–98
  (*See also* Dot commands)
Comment lines:
  dot command for, 73
  saving ruler lines as, 30
Control characters:
  for hiding superscripts, 48–51
  in search and replace operations, 92
Copying:
  blocks, 94–95
  files, 17
Cursor:
  commands for, 6–9
  quick menu for control of, 19
  status line indication of location of, 4
Cursor control keys, 7

# Command Index

The commands listed in this index are in alphabetical order. The commands available from the opening menu are listed first, followed by the commands that can be used during editing. For the commands that can be used during editing, the single-letter commands are given first, two-letter commands next, and dot commands last. After each command is the page number or numbers where the command can be found in the book.

**Commands Available from the Opening Menu**   To access these commands, the opening menu must be on the screen. The letters you type for the commands do not have to be uppercase.

| Command | Function | Page(s) |
|---------|----------|---------|
| D | Open a document file | 3, 15 |
| E | Rename a file | 17 |
| F | File directory on or off | 14 |
| H | Set help level | 14 |
| L | Change logged disk drive | 14 |
| M | Run MailMerge | 16 |
| N | Open a nondocument file | 3, 15 |
| O | Copy a file | 17 |
| P | Print a file | 16, 34 |
| R | Run a program | 15 |
| S | Run SpellStar | 16 |
| X | Exit to system | 16 |
| Y | Delete a file | 17 |

**Single-Letter Commands to Use during Editing**    Each of the following commands can be used during editing. In each case the CONTROL key must be held down while the letter of the command is typed. The command letter does not have to be uppercase. Note that commands not followed by a page number are commands not covered in this book. In most cases their function is self-explanatory.

| Command | Function | Page(s) |
|---------|----------|---------|
| ^A | Cursor left one word | 7 |
| ^B | Re-form paragraph | 10, 25 |
| ^C | Scroll screen down one screen | 8 |
| ^D | Cursor right one character | 7 |
| ^E | Cursor up one character | 7 |
| ^F | Cursor right one word | 7 |
| ^G | Delete a character | 11 |
| ^H | Delete character to left of cursor | — |
| ^I | Tab | — |
| ^J | Display the help menu | 20 |
| ^K | Display the block menu | 19 |
| ^L | Find again | 89 |
| ^M | Same as return | — |
| ^N | Insert "hard" carriage return | — |
| ^O | Display the onscreen menu | 18, 23 |
| ^P | Display the print menu | 18 |
| ^Q | Display the quick menu | 19 |
| ^R | Scroll screen up one screen | 8 |
| ^S | Cursor left one character | 7 |
| ^T | Delete a word | 11 |
| ^U | Interrupt command in progress | — |
| ^V | INSERT on/off | 9 |
| ^W | Scroll screen up one line | 8 |
| ^X | Cursor down one character | 7 |
| ^Y | Delete a line | 11 |
| ^Z | Scroll screen down one line | 8 |

**Two-Letter Commands to Use during Editing**    To give any of the following commands, you must hold down the CONTROL key while the first letter is typed. The second letter can be typed with or without the CONTROL key. Neither of the letters must be a capital.

| Command | Function | Page(s) |
|---------|----------|---------|
| ^JH | Set help level | — |
| ^KB | Mark the beginning of a block | 12, 93 |
| ^KC | Copy marked block | 13, 94 |
| ^KD | Save and return to opening menu | 5 |
| ^KE | Rename a file | — |
| ^KF | File directory on/off | — |
| ^KH | Hide block markers | 13, 95 |
| ^KJ | Delete a file | — |
| ^KK | Mark end of block | 12, 93 |
| ^KN | Column mode on/off | 95 |
| ^KP | Print a file | 34 |
| ^KQ | Abandon file | — |

**Dot Commands**  The dot (or period) in each dot command must be in column 1. Any characters on the same line as a dot command will be ignored during printing. With most dot commands, a number or a string of characters is specified after the dot command. Also, a number of these dot commands cannot be interpreted by dot-matrix printers.

| Command | Function | Page(s) |
|---|---|---|
| .BP # | Bidirectional print on/off<br>If # = 1, ON; if # = 0, OFF | 73 |
| .CP # | Begin new page if less than # lines are left on the current page | 72 |
| .CW # | $^{\#}/_{120}$ inches per character<br>Default for # is 12 | 61 |
| .FO | Footing line is<br>Leave one space and type text to appear at bottom of each page | 66 |
| .FM # | # blank lines between last possible line of text and footing<br>Default for # is 2 | 70 |
| .HE | Heading line is<br>Leave one space and type text to appear at top of each page | 66 |
| .HM # | # blank lines between heading and beginning of text<br>Default for # is 2 | 69 |
| .IG | Ignore this line | 73 |
| .LH # | Line height $^{\#}/_{48}$ inches per line<br>Default for # is 8 | 60 |
| .MT # | Top margin is # lines<br>Default for # is 3 | 63 |
| .MB # | Bottom margin is # lines<br>Default for # is 8 | 63 |
| .OP | Omit page numbers | 60 |
| .PA | Begin new page | 70 |
| .PC # | Page number in column #<br>Default for # is 33 | 60 |
| .PL # | Page length is # lines<br>Default for # is 66 | 64 |
| .PO # | Begin printing in column #<br>Default for # is 8 | 64 |
| .PN # | Number pages beginning with # | 60 |
| .SR # | Superscript/subscript roll $^{\#}/_{48}$ inch<br>Default for # is 3 | 57, 72 |
| .UJ # | Microjustification on/off<br>If # = 1, ON; if # = 0, OFF | 72 |

## About the Author

Charles "Pat" McKeague teaches mathematics at Cuesta College in San Luis Obispo, California. He is also the author of several leading college mathematics texts. This book grew out of his experiences in using WordStar to author his texts.